GOVERNMENT

of

HOPE

Blueprint for Reformation:
A New World Awaits

Joey LeTourneau

Dedication:

To ALL those who have sown into our lives and journey making it possible for this blueprint to come together, and hopefully, come to life. There are too many of you to name, we trust that you know who you are. We certainly do. Thank you!

Acknowledgments:

Chuck and Doretha, the time away at your home helped us get this project moving, thank you! Thanks to Colleen Kuehter and Michael Kuehter for your editing expertise. Michele and Ken, your prayers and support are beyond faithful. To Jeffrey & Caryn Beth for that special and timely word that helped confirm this project. Garris, thanks for great espresso and far better company & conversation. Dan & Ava, thank you for everything! Cameron, thanks for walking so closely with me during this "governmental" season, and always. Josh Brewer, for running & building with us. The Shattucks & Buchanans, for going after this 'family structure' with us! The Goodsons, Majors, Carsons, Shareen and Bev for being community up here amidst this all. The Mullis', Wilburns, Stones, Blackmons, Blasers, Carters, Cross', Hunter and Jason & Debby for your incredible friendship & support. Annie & Mike, there are no words for your prayers and support. John & Terina; for always being there, believing and helping make our mission and calling possible. And to my family (again, too many to mention) who have prayed for and supported me, us, and this project unconditionally, with faith, hope and love. *Thank you!*

Endorsement:

Joey LeTourneau's book "Government of Hope" is a key for this new era we have entered. It is not only a key, it is a deep well of revelation, impartation and hope. This book calls the people of God higher. This challenges the Church to come deeper into intimacy with Jesus and to live from our seat (Ephesians 2:6) and see His government established on the earth. This book carries a deep impartation of hope and faith and will activate you into your destiny in the earth in greater ways and draw you deeper into His heart of love and awaken you in deeper ways to the sound of reformation that is resounding from His heart. It's time to take your place in the earth like never before and Joey's book will be a tool and a key to assist you in your positioning.

Lana Vawser
Founder Lana Vawser Ministries
Author, Speaker, Prophetic Voice
lanavawser.com

Table of Contents:

Table of Contents

Foreword:

If you are like me, the word "hope" is not what I would attach as a descriptor to the subject of government. This is why I find this book by Joey LeTourneau to be such a gem. More than ever, we need someone to present another option to us instead of continuing into the future hopelessly gridlocked in partisan politics. *Government of Hope*, by its very title, is a call to attention and a reminder that with God, all things are possible.

Joey and I have known each other for several years. Recently, I sat across a table from Joey on several visits and processed the issue of hope in the arena of politics. As I listened to Joey unpack his ideas, I was refreshed and encouraged. As you get to know the heart of Joey LeTourneau, you will come to realize his voice is prophetic, not political. He is announcing the possibility of doing government in a new and refreshing way.

The LeTourneau family has lived and served in very challenging posts around the world. In each instance, they breathed hope into hopeless situations. Their values have been the blueprint of their family life - a life of hope. Under that blueprint of hope, despair turned to joy, and sorrow became rejoicing. Hope is the pen Joey used to author this book. As I read through the pages, I recalled my conversations with Joey. I heard his voice. I came away after reading *Government of Hope* with hope in a new possibility for the future, and I believe as you read this book, you will come away with that same hope.

- Garris Elkins

Garris Elkins is an author, mentor, and speaker. He writes and speaks prophetically on the heart of God and the reformation of culture. Garris and his wife live in Southern Oregon.

Introduction: It's Time

It's time! I can't stop saying those words. I believe that right now our world is as ready as ever for us, followers of Jesus, to carry out the increase of the government and peace that He ushered into the world. We are venturing into new territory, and though the wind and waves may surround us, though this new world might not be what we expected, this is the time to take our hope back from the political world we live in and be the government of hope God's family has always been created to be.

Though some of this book is written in American context, it applies and is intended for the nations as a whole. The reality is that whomever we are, wherever we are, whatever we do or do not have; we honor our government and the protections and freedom it offers, yet we use the fullness of our freedom to show the world another way, *The Way* that is alive in us, ready to offer solutions that are more than left vs. right, or red vs. blue. It's time for us to be the government that God intended His family structure to provide.

The world has many counterfeits, but the kingdom of God carries the only true hope. This book is not written merely for an idea, but to offer a blueprint of how we can come together in sync and in tune with the Spirit of God to offer the world a grassroots government that exudes hope, freedom, generosity, true identity, empowering the least of these, and belonging to the greatest family on earth.

We can be—*we are*—that blueprint! And now is the time for us to bring it to life. This reformation of governing hope looks like something that is both familiar, and yet something that is still unfulfilled; God's government looks like a revolution of *family*.

Chapter 1:

Venturing Into A New World

> "For unto us a child is born, unto us a Son is given; and the government will be upon His shoulder. And His name will be called Wonderful, Counselor, Mighty God, Everlasting Father, Prince of Peace. Of the increase of His government and peace there will be no end..." (Isaiah 9:6-7, NKJV)

As the star shined that night over Bethlehem to point the way, the most pure government ever was born on the shoulders of a baby in a manger, destined for its increase. That government is the one that's alive within us, and it's greater—and different—than the one to which our politics subscribe.

Neither red nor blue is the color of hope or change. And that "baby" is now fulfilled and mature for such a time as this—waiting to be lived out *through* us in an upside-down, grass roots government that serves and empowers others while many in the world scheme to gain power for themselves.

My family and I spent three memorable months living on the outskirts of Bethlehem, right in line with the Shepherd's fields where that star pointed so brightly. I'll never forget the power of walking out on our patio at night, looking up and realizing that these were the very stars which shined over this small rural area that birthed our Savior, His government, and the possibilities that were at that moment conceived.

It wasn't a tourist attraction that buses pulled up to visit, and I don't even know if I have a photo to remember it by; but my soul and spirit will always frame it for me: this most unlikely environment was the birthplace of the greatest government of them all. And it's time for such a government to come more fully alive through us today.

Out of these ordinary fields came the Servant-Ruler who redefines which government we depend on, and what "ruling" really looks like. If the manger under those stars was the unlikely qualification, then I had better begin to open my blind eyes not only to *see* where His government of true hope is ready to arise from today, but to *believe*. Before we go on I have to ask you one simple question: *Do you believe?*

"For you see your calling, brethren, that not many wise according to the flesh, not many mighty, not many noble, are called. But God has chosen the foolish things of the world to put to shame the wise, and God has chosen the weak things of the world to put to shame the things which are mighty; and the base things of the world and the things which are despised God has chosen, and the things which are not, to bring to nothing the things that are, that no flesh should glory in his presence..." (1 Corinthians 1:26-30)

Do you believe that God still uses the foolish things to confound the wise? Do you believe that God still chooses the weak things of the world to put to shame the things which are mighty? Do you truly believe that God uses, even chooses, the base things and that which are despised to bring about the hope and change that we have been praying for? Do you believe that God still uses "Manger Strategies" to bring about His divine purpose? Do you believe that He's ready to do it again?

Do you believe that in this time in the world, amid the current tug-o-war power struggle of partisan politics all around us, that we have present day "Bethlehems" and "Nazareths"— places, people and other unlikely sources—where a government of true hope can arise from? Do you believe you could be part of such government that is genuinely for the people—all people— and brought about *by* the people? Or can you see the "stars" that point to those who will?

I do.

I believe.

I believe that is where we find Jesus' government of hope that He ushered in on His shoulders. It now resides in us and in many of the people, places and strategies which seem to have no earthly strength, likelihood, or even hope. Where there seems to be no hope is often the very birthplace of hope itself. We often know this, yet still fall back depending on more known, tangible earthly powers and influence to fulfill the world's great needs.

We have to go beyond simply knowing. We have to invest— consistently— our time, treasures, talents, and most importantly our trust, into those "base things" of the world, as that is there we will find what the star was pointing to that night. We have to journey like the shepherds, kings and wise men into a new world, a new paradigm, where the power structures and political structures are confounded by this living government that is the only kind that can truly give the world the free gifts it is desperate for.

Right now, partisan politics have taken our dependence and our trust. Our words and beliefs say one thing, but our *consistent* actions have too often said another. In which government will we truly place our hope? Which government will we *be* for the world? We don't need earthly power, influence or a platform for such a government; God is willing to birth a miracle of hope out of whatever you have in your hands—that's His specialty. He takes what we call our nothing, the very nothing we sometimes ask our national government to provide for, and He turns it into something mighty for us and for others.

We absolutely must still honor and faithfully vote for the natural structure of government and our leaders, as they help provide us freedoms to live out this other government of hope. But while doing so, we must check where we are placing our dependence and where we are placing our hope. Once we re-calibrate ourselves, that is where we begin to invest our tangible and intangible resources with the same certainty in the unseen that we naturally place in those things that are seen. We must once again find a government that is alive in our breath and our belly, a government that doesn't come to be served, but to serve; a government *through* the people and not just for them.

As culture is divided and many look for hope in political answers, there is an authentic answer to the counterfeits currently arising in culture—a layered answer that rings prophetic within JFK's famous quote:

> *"Ask not what your country can do for you, but what you can do for your country."* - *John F. Kennedy Jr.*

Personally, my family and I just finished one of the most unique experiences of our lives and calling: running for the U.S. House of Representatives in northern California. But we didn't run a very typical race. For a number of years I sensed something of a "governmental call" from the Lord. I never knew if it would be literal or more spiritually speaking. I've had specific words and encouragements spoken into my life and family from the Lord, and people, and have always felt a draw or connection to those like Joseph, Daniel, Zerubbabel and the like. But I can't say that I had specifically planned on running for Congress.

But one day early this last fall, all the dots connected and we believed we were supposed to run, and run not so much for an office as much as with a message that would impact culture. We didn't want to be in power, we wanted to serve and empower. We wanted to take power back from politics again and give it to people so that they could have the freedom and courage to live out a government of true hope. And yet, this step into this unknown political world of government would require a new level of courage for myself and my family as well.

At the beginning I would wake up and it would feel very foreign, like I was David wearing Saul's armor. This was always a great reminder not to put on the world's expectations for what our campaign should look like, but to feel free to be authentic and to engage in this battle with whom God has made us to be. My favorite part of the campaign was the daily dependence on God and running this race with Him. I had to receive our marching order, when to step and when to stop, from Him. I couldn't react to the world's expectations or pressures or else that would give power back to the political and the typical.

How I ran mattered much more than whether or not I would win. I could not see the government we hoped for come alive if we subscribed to the usual process as we cannot do the same things while expecting a different result. The only way to see change would be to change the way we went about our day-to-day campaign, regardless of what that meant. And sometimes, it was very uncomfortable. Most of the time, it was incredibly rewarding and such an intimate process *with* God. I had to consistently come face to face with the question that decides where our hope is anchored: *Where am I putting my trust?*

Though I come from conservative values, we ran for office to be prophetic, not political. We wanted to take government back from politics again, so we ran as "Independent" or "No Party Preference" because it was most authentic to our voice.

We ran for reformation, to put people before politics again, to go beyond the issues that divide us, and to point the way forward while healing the roots of our culture. Though we weren't successful in winning our election, the morning after I still felt so much victory because something new had been born. The election or position wasn't the baby or promise being born. Rather, our campaign, for us, was the process of labor and delivery to help bring a new, yet ancient and necessary government to life for the time we are now living in.

Five Branches of Hope's Government:

> **"For unto us a child is born, unto us a Son is given; and the government will be upon His shoulder. And His name will be called Wonderful, Counselor, Mighty God, Everlasting Father, Prince of Peace. Of the increase of His government and peace there will be no end..." (Isaiah 9:6-7)**

When I read those words, "And His name will be called..." I am struck that we are in that time of "will be"—past the time, really—the time when the increase of His government will be ushered in under the pillars of these names that "He will be called." We in America adhere to and honor the three branches of our government: the Executive Branch, the Judicial Branch and the Legislative Branch. But I wonder, perhaps, if the following names better represent the government of hope that our nation and world really need now.

Wonderful:

Sadly, it is not often in our culture that we are filled with genuine wonder any more. We have little that can't be explained by science or statistics, and that which cannot be often gets thrown out as foolish. But there is that "foolishness" again. There is that place that returns us to a childlike nature which Jesus Himself said ushers in the kingdom (Mark 10:14).

We will not learn to "wonder" again if we do not put ourselves in a position to do so. We won't marvel with wonder at God if we do not give Him room within our trust and dependence. Sometimes believing God can show up and do something amazing, something miraculous, isn't enough if we do not also demonstrate our trust by giving Him room to do so.

The Bible shows us in both New and Old Testament that God is always a God of signs and wonders; how much so usually depends on how much room we make for Him. It's hard to make that room when we depend more on the economy or specific legislation than we do upon God. The world cannot return to the "wonder" it marveled with throughout the Bible without people who don't have all the answers. And that is exactly what the world needs.

Counselor:

One of my favorite things about King David, whose line our Heavenly Government flows through, is that he so often inquired of the Lord. The Lord was His counselor. Therefore, the people naturally became privy to God's counsel as well. We have come to make government about "the issues" of our time. Many of these are real issues, but most are being exploited by the agendas of partisan politics. If we are going to usher in an authentic government of lasting change we will have to go beyond the surface of issues and seek healing for our culture at its roots.

We will need counsel full of tried and tested wisdom and revelation more than just answers, opinions or sides. We need the kind of solutions that those like Joseph or Daniel understood that aren't tinted red or blue, but which come from the heart of God, who knows how to surgically enter and knit the seam that stitches the wounds and gapes of both sides back into a place of wholeness, above rightness.

Mighty God:

We won't learn to give God our trust or make ourselves dependent on Him if we do not actually believe that He is who He says He is: a *Mighty God*. We have to know His character, and His word, for only then will we have the faith of Abraham who was **"fully convinced that what He (God) had promised He was also able to perform. And therefore it was accounted to him for righteousness." (Romans 4:21-22).**

We may sing about the Mighty God we serve, but when was the last time we allowed Him to be that in our lives? Don't get me wrong, our faith requires our deeds and we partner and co-labor with God to bring about His kingdom. But there is both give and take in that living relationship and sometimes we are trying so hard to prove "mighty" ourselves, or trust in a power or might that we can see that we do not call Him this name with our faith.

There is no government of hope without actively having our Mighty God with us, for us, and through us. We cannot be vessels of generosity, of life, liberty or peace without the Mighty God being given the faith to flow through our lives. And when we

12

allow ourselves to personally experience the freshness of His might, we will never want to go back to mere man's ways for our answers again. We have no government to offer if we don't learn to actively trust a living and Mighty God.

Everlasting Father:

There are so many layers to the world's need for the Everlasting Father. We live in a world where fatherlessness is a hidden cancer unknowingly affecting all that we do. Unlike other needs in our world that we are forthright about, more than ever our culture aches for us to answer the need that it won't often enough ask for: fathers and mothers. That's what politics needs, what our government needs, what our schools and universities need, what our media and modern culture lack: *fathers and mothers*. I always love the words of Jesus when speaking to Phillip in John 14:9:

> **"Have I been with you so long, Phillip? He who has seen Me has seen the Father; so how can you say, 'Show us the Father?'"**

I pray we can bring about a consistent day-to-day government of hope where we *all* can begin to genuinely say, *"If you've seen me, you've seen the Father."*

Prince of Peace:

This one might be the most important to the practical template of us learning to offer the world a government of hope. As we all know, we have hard times and troubles in this world. Sometimes they are personal struggles, and sometimes, like the COVID-19 pandemic, they are also corporate battles and needs.

In John 16:33 Jesus assured us that in the world we will have these troubles, but also that He has overcome the world.

The idea behind Prince of Peace, when translated from the original Hebrew word *Sar Shalom*, or "The Prince of Shalom", becomes more than just about peace. To better understand the government of hope that we can bring to the world around us we can unlock the depth and power of the word "shalom" itself. Shalom actually means:

"Completeness, wholeness, peace, health, welfare, safety, soundness, tranquility, prosperity, perfectness, fullness, rest, harmony; the absence of agitation or discord."

The "Word Wealth" notes in my Bible says of shalom that it *"is much more than the absence of war and conflict; it is the wholeness that the entire human race seeks."*

Let's note together the power in that last sentence. **Shalom is the wholeness that the entire human race seeks.** And He lives in us. Perhaps you also notice that many of these definitions are exactly what we typically look to our government to provide for us. This is how we have allowed the government to take the place of God in many aspects of our lives and culture, facets of hope from God's government that we are supposed to live and give to the world.

We often quote the verse, *"Christ in us, the hope of glory."* That also means, *The Prince of Peace* in us, the hope of glory. We have living inside of us what the world is hoping the government can or will provide them. Health. Welfare. Safety. Prosperity. Sound familiar? I venture to say we've heard all those and more argued across debate stages and as promises that are filling up political ads.

We have in the Prince of Peace within us the fullness of each of those areas that people are literally in need of every day. We will have a government of hope when we realize that, and when we depend on God to provide such for us, and through us, on a daily basis.

What if we took all the time and energy that we put in the right or the left, into the red, or the blue, and put it into this "based," "despised," "weak," "foolish," unseen government that will only be seen when we invest our hope in it more than other good but lesser forms?

Amidst the great divide in our nation—and world—we must refrain from just choosing a side, rather, we must recognize that perhaps the giant caveat of a dividing line between us didn't use to be a dividing line at all. It used to be the path forward, until we turned sideways on one another. With it, our hope for change has gone sideways and we are trying to win the tug-o-war to find it again, often for good motives, but it is pertinent now that we turn our eyes again on the horizon ahead, re-take perspective, and transform the dividing line going through culture back into the leading path it once was.

Stepping onto this path is how we show the world the narrow way forward again. We re-set the vision of where we place our trust and then we begin, together, to mobilize a true government of hope for the world to experience through our lives.

Chapter 2:

The Revolutionary Way

> "The Spirit of the Lord is upon Me, because He has anointed Me to preach the gospel to the poor; He has sent Me to heal the brokenhearted, to proclaim liberty to the captives and recovery of sight to the blind, to set at liberty those who are oppressed; To proclaim the acceptable year of the Lord." (Luke 4:18-19)

Before we venture into more of what this government of hope will look like, it's imperative that we look at the revolutionary "way" that leads us into such living blueprints.

In the movie, *Amazing Grace*, William Wilberforce continues steadfastly to fight against the social norm of slavery when one of his opponents in the House of Commons jabs back with this rebuttal: "Revolution is like the pox, it spreads from person to person." And unfortunately, that is what we typically try and do with even the most noble of revolutionary leaders and ideas; we treat them like the pox and, for fear of them, we place them in quarantine to protect the safe status quo from the unmitigated life and liberty that could become something of an epidemic that goes beyond our control.

We should not be afraid of revolution. And we shouldn't lose our honor for the government or the leaders of the status quo. But we do need to let go of our dependence upon them. William Wilberforce, one of my longtime heroes, had to go against the grain of culture, with God, without compromise to help society soar past the quarantine that traditionalists or even common sense would have put him, or abolition within. Common sense is a necessary commodity, but at the same time I do not believe Jesus has called our mindsets, nor our actions, to be very common. And yet among all the detractors of the revolutionary way, most are not fierce opposition of good. Rather, they are more often than not fearful of the uncommon package that surrounds the new, and the change that they themselves may have even been praying for.

Wilberforce had to be free from both the applause of man and the ridicule of man. He had to be free so that others could have their freedom. That is what the revolutionary way is all about. It's an internal freedom and a renewed mindset that empowers us beyond the boundaries of the known good and into the fiery prayers we've long petitioned.

Wilberforce's detractor in that House of Commons was correct. Revolution really is like the pox in that one way, that it spreads from person to person. And that is exactly what we need from a government of hope. We need people across the board that will pick up their freedom and learn to fly again.

"Freedom is never more than one generation away from extinction. We didn't pass it on to our children in the bloodstream. It must be fought for, protected, and handed on for them to do the same." - Ronald Reagan

Dream, Again

The following passage is from a book I authored (<u>Dream, Again</u>, pg. 3) about re-interpreting the American dream. This specific passage (and much of the book) is written from the perspective of a character named, *Founder*, a bald eagle that is essentially the personified mascot of America.

"My name is Founder. You may have met me from a distance in any number of places, the dollar bill, or any variety of seals and crests still littered across our great nation. My family line enthroned me as the symbol of a freedom whose truth has become scarce these days, a means vs. an end, a lone, high perch plucked for the price of trading in our wings. I've got the scars to prove it. And my wings, that which could have actually lifted me higher than that forsaken perch, were nearly lost in the process.

I became comfortable you see, and abandoned my pioneering edge. I once danced upon the skies with the greatest of freedom, led by unparalleled vision, yet even the quality of such esteemed traits weren't enough to keep me from blending in captive to the culture of the wolves. Their lure was subtle, and their prowess for deception had kept me blind. I was lost inside myself long before those stripes of blood threatened to permanently dismember my freedom. But, if not for those scars and stripes, I wouldn't be qualified to lead you today."

The American dream didn't used to be about the self-comforts or esteemed places our freedom could get us, it was about freedom itself. The dream was to have and use our wings, not to be the bronzed statue of a freedom that was just accomplished and entitled, but to actually fly! Now, too often, we're afraid of falling from the perch we've long been hoisted to and nestled upon and we've forgotten the revolutionary way, the wings that are still by our sides.

We were created to soar, not to just maintain what the heights of what those who've gone before us captured, but to spread our wings like they did and use our freedom before we lose it. That is what this nation, and the world, need most right now.

William Penn

This sort of liberty, both governmental and religious, is what America was founded upon and it has had many faces leading its revolution over the years. One well-known but too little understood pioneer of such liberties before America even became a nation is William Penn. We know him from afar because of those things like the state of Pennsylvania, a university with his namesake and the like. But there is so much more to know of his revolutionary spirit of liberty that may have raised a raucous in his day but is celebrated now.

For me, it isn't just about what Penn established, but how he did so. Once that fire was lit in him, many tried to quell it, even his own father and especially the Church of England, but he held true and kept moving forward through pressures and persecutions.

It was Penn's newly found Quaker faith that spurred him on, refusing to bow down his oath or number one loyalty to the throne or the form of Christianity that came with it. Ahead of his time, Penn was a revolutionary in the moment that turned out to be a founder of religious liberty and a pioneer of the governing structure we all enjoy today. He is a ringing example of one who went against the grain of societal or cultural standards to call a prophetic version of freedom and what it could be, into the here and now.

Penn was a Quaker who followed and obeyed his "inner light," which they believed came directly from God. It was a radical form of faith in that day whose principles differed greatly from the state imposed religion. He was persecuted and jailed for his refusal to swear an oath to state and religious governance, holding fast to the belief that his first oath was to God and that according to Matthew 5:34 he was not to swear such oath to anyone, or anything. Penn stated,

"If thou wouldst rule well, then thou must rule for God, and to do that, thou must be ruled by him. Those who will not be governed by God will be ruled by tyrants."
- William Penn

He was rather prophetic if I do say so myself as we now face many of the hard realities of his piercing words. He was deemed a revolutionary, not a compliment back in that day, but precisely what our hope needs now. Looking for liberty to live their beliefs, Penn was among a group of Quakers that in 1677 received the Colonial Province of West New Jersey. Penn himself helped draft a charter of liberties for the settlement in which he guaranteed free and fair trial by jury, freedom of religion, freedom from unjust imprisonment and free elections—concepts that are familiar to us, even expected today—but principles that had to be pursued passionately by those like Penn.

Penn was later granted land on American soil by King Charles II due to a debt the King owed Penn's father, land that would become something of a "Holy Experiment" for Penn. This land would become what we know today as Pennsylvania. Penn was full of new political ideas and ways to build society based on his faith and principles of liberty. He put together plans for a city of brotherly love, Philadelphia. He put his reformative ideas into workable form to construct the state, and the city upon new ideas small and large. His revolutionary ways suddenly became foundational for a new era, and a new land.

Penn was true to his beliefs and ahead of his time in that he would make agreements to acquire further land instead of typical methods of conquest. He befriended the local Native Americans, the Leni-Lenape-Delaware tribe and ensured fair payment for the land. Penn even went so far as to learn several native language dialects so he personally could communicate with the leaders in negotiation. He instituted fair trials for the natives and proved successful in creating peace with the natives, unlike most colonies. The writer, Voltaire, praised Penn's *"Great Treaty"* as "the only treaty between those people (Indians & Europeans) that was not ratified by an oath, and that was never infringed" (*U.S. History.org*). The colonists of Pennsylvania and the natives remained at peace much longer than in other colonies and the treaty was so revolutionary that many would still even call it a myth.

The true myth of our day has become this type of revolutionary freedom. It rarely feels rewarded in the moment, as if you are constantly pressing up against worldly pressure and opposition. But with Jesus, we can stand firm on a living, forward moving faith in the promised authority He has given us to take such new ground:

> "Blessed are you, Simon Bar-Jonah, for flesh and blood has not revealed this to you but My Father who is in heaven. And I also say to you that you are Peter, and on this rock I will build my church, and the gates of Hades shall not prevail against it." (Matthew 16:17-18)

Peter was blessed for his revolutionary faith. It hadn't been handed to him, but he recognized the living nature of Christ. When we give ourselves to such a living nature, we cannot help but become revolutionary like Him. And the territory that the enemy currently possesses will not prevail against those who press forward to take this new ground and see His government established.

Jesus of Nazareth

> "The Spirit of the Lord is upon Me, because He has anointed Me to preach the gospel to the poor; He has sent Me to heal the brokenhearted, to proclaim liberty to the captives and recovery of sight to the blind, to set at liberty those who are oppressed; To proclaim the acceptable year of the Lord." (Luke 4:18-19)

When Jesus stepped forward in the synagogue in Nazareth to read this passage from the book of Isaiah, chapter 61, He was proclaiming a freedom, a revolutionary freedom that He Himself epitomized in order to offer that same kind of liberty to the world.

That moment, though familiar to us now was more revolutionary than we could ever know. That simply was *not* how you did things back then. That was not what, *ahem*, "ministry" looked like. Jesus was going against the grain of culture by unapologetically announcing Who He was and what He was there to do. It was a pivotal and necessary moment in bringing forth the government of heaven and showing what it would require to live such a government out to those in need.

Walking into that church in Nazareth where Jesus declared those revolutionary words was one of the few tourist sites we actually went out of our way to visit, navigating Nazareth's small zig-zagging streets trying to find our way. I went to the front of the church to join my Lord in reading that portion of Isaiah 61 aloud, only imagining the fierce pressure He stood through, humble yet steadfast; and by faith receiving that anointing on our own lives as well. It was, after all, the title and subject matter of one of my first books, Revolutionary Freedom: The Declaration of Isaiah 61—and a primary theme in our lives. Thus, it was a personal moment I'll always cherish.

Upon leaving that poignant site we continued the path of Jesus' revolutionary way when we drove up to the edge of Mt. Precipice where the people went a few steps beyond quarantine, seeking to march our Lord up the mountain intending to throw Him over the cliff because of the heretical nature of the proclamation He had just made. Not exactly a receptive audience. Yet, neither will we be able to bring a true government of hope into the world if we ourselves will not stand up against the status quo and the fear of man that seeks to intimidate what it itself is afraid of.

Sometimes that status quo is found in a certain cultural norm, and sometimes it is found within our own familiar or comfortable patterns inside of us. Both need to be broken through. The reality is that Jesus was paving the revolutionary way for us, giving us the freedom to be different, to lift up our wings and fly once again. Giving us the freedom to withstand the pressures of man, to break the mold or be the first one through the wall and take new ground.

Jesus was free to be misunderstood, and to trust the Father in the process. Jesus had so much liberty inside Him that He was the picture and the way of the revolutionary. He did so with honor, not just abolishing the old but fulfilling it while guiding all who would receive it into the new. And that is the kind of freedom we too must learn if we want to give the world the whole government that the Son carried upon His shoulders into that manger.

This revolutionary way is a part of essential liberty. It is part of the process in discovering such liberty, keeping such liberty, and in reviving it again. It was a kind of liberty that America's forefathers themselves walked in so they could secure it for this great country, for you and I today. And if America will keep her essential liberty intact against the many threats moving in; it will be because a new wave of revolutionaries stood up to the fear of the times and won a different kind of battle than what they fought then.

Such liberty is a choice more than an achievement, though. I've often looked back on the Revolutionary War and thought about how formally out-manned America was against the British. It was a war that, on paper, they probably wouldn't have achieved on their own merit. I've always believed that the revolutionaries won that war when they decided they needed their own nation to follow God as their King. They chose God and freedom, and the victory was the grace we all were given because of such choice.

We are in a day and time when that choice is needed again. We cannot sit back entitled to what we won, rather we need to realize the revolutionary choices they made and make a stand of our own. We need to take a revolutionary stance against fear, against lies, against greed and selfishness, entitlement, apathy, and once again become a people who blaze a trail of a fresh government who know that we have something new, something needed, and something special to offer because of Who lives in us and what His government has always been about. We need to make choices that aren't just to preserve the comforts of what other revolutionaries chose and fought for, and choices for the convictions we want to pass down to the world. I want to give my kids a government of hope.

However, the ironic thing about change or something new, is it usually requires something new to get there. Therein lies the problem, and there lies the revolutionary way.

River Life

I want to wrap up this chapter with another portion from my book _Dream, Again_, because it paints a picture and brings to life one of my favorite descriptions of what the revolutionary way can feel like. It is the path and nature of a river amid a world being sung lullaby's of stagnancy.

> _"The river is the ultimate pioneer. If you want to take back the pioneering spirit that confounds the wolves you and your family are feeling, learn the river. For the river lives and moves and breathes—wherever it goes. It gives life while also taking new ground. The river is the picture of the path of a pioneer. It may look unsafe in its twists, turns and the varying seasons and terrain it unpredictably encounters moving forward, but when you are found in the river there is not a safer place on earth._

The wolves stay far from here, and us eagles find it to be some of the most hospitable life there is...It is not just a place, it's a lifestyle, a culture of life that never stops breathing, that allows whose who are hurting and dying for refreshment to take a deep breath or drink. Too many people trade the river's appearance of insecurity and unpredictability while looking for ponds of assurance to fill the insecurity deep within their own lives and thoughts. One takes new ground all around you, and the other takes away ground from within you. One is a culture of pioneers, and the other a culture of wolves. The way of the river is not always easy, but rest assured that over the long haul, it is the most secure. It is what your nation was found upon, and what it must return to if they will ever learn to dream, again." (pgs. 104-105)

"Two roads diverged in the woods and I—I took the one less traveled by, and that made all the difference." - Robert Frost

Chapter 3:

The Mayflower Compact

A few months back during a time of transition I was asking the Lord for a clear word or picture of what was ahead. I was walking down the stairs of our previous home and was surprised to hear what I believe was the Lord whispering faintly in my heart: *"Mayflower."*

Now, on the surface I could see no reason why the Mayflower would be important to where we were at that time. In fact, the only thing I could think of was the moving company that goes by that name, and though we were moving, it was only a re-location down the street.

So, I began to go back to study and refresh myself on all things Mayflower. In doing so I was drawn to two different elements: 1. *Mayflower* was a vessel that carried people into a new world. 2. *The Mayflower Compact* was a temporary or provisional government formed by the Pilgrims after their landing spot was different than had been planned, therefore throwing off mutual agreements among passengers of the ship and creating a time of division and discord.

This temporary government helped them come together to navigate their entrance into a new era, and a new land. It was short and simple, but this social sort of government among them served them well and became a foundation for our nation today. It was written as follows (*from History.com, The Mayflower*):

> "In the name of God, Amen. We, whose names are underwritten, the Loyal Subjects of our dread Sovereign Lord King James, by the Grace of God, of Great Britain, France, and Ireland, King, defender of the Faith, etc.:
>
> Having undertaken, for the Glory of God, and advancements of the Christian faith, and the honor of our King and Country, a voyage to plant the first colony in the Northern parts of Virginia; do by these presents, solemnly and mutually, in the presence of God, and one another; covenant and combine ourselves together, into a civil body politic; for our better ordering, and preservation and furtherance of the ends aforesaid: and by virtue here of to enact, constitute, and frame, such just and equal laws, ordinances, acts, constitutions, and offices, from time to time, as shall be though most meet and convenient for the general good of the colony: unto which we promise all due submission and obedience."

I believe the Mayflower Compact to be a model for what our culture and world needs right now, and what we as believers must come together within. I think it can remind us of how we can come together in a grassroots type of government outside the walls of each of our existing, known structures, across society, while still founded upon God and freedom, for the furtherance of our faith. It shows us that we can still create a new socially empowering construct of free government without bowing to the cries for socialism.

This government of hope we're shining light upon is a similar type of provisional, socially led, grassroots government like the covenant that those Pilgrims made, built upon the covenant that Jesus Himself sealed. It helps the people to navigate and establish new principles of living as we cross through a time of discord and enter into a new era of hope, and harvest!

The Pilgrims sailed aboard the Mayflower towards Virginia with specific plans in mind, but when they landed far enough north to disrupt those arrangements they found themselves in unknown territory and at odds with one another. Venturing to a new land, many must have been fearful, while others fought to regain control. I think many of us would attest we have battles going on around us in the world that are causing much of the same. They needed a new way forward, and so do we. As believers we've already been given the very government the world so badly needs right now, and it's time for us to bring it to life more fully.

In essence, they cultivated a grassroots government of hope; a government called forth and lived out from a place in their soul, an inner plumb line that superseded their individual rights for justice they could have legally held to. The Mayflower Compact may have been a "temporary" government, but in truth it was superior in its living framework and helped them pioneer into God's new and special purposes.

I believe we have been given the invitation to board our own Mayflower in this day and age, and it will require a revolutionary, living government of hope that gives more than it requires. Our nation is venturing into a new era and we have arrived in a time that doesn't appear to add up to our expected destination.

So what do we do? We rediscover the government of hope that supersedes the world's ways we have for too long bowed our kingdom government to. We honor our nation's government, but we choose to subscribe to and live out a seemingly unseen government that will know no end. Where is it that this boat has taken us? And what is the charge this government of hope gives us to live out? We are venturing across the world and back to the beginning, where true hope can and will be found in the simplest, yet often the hardest forms. These are not laws that we legislate, but a life that we freely live, and give.

Similar to William Penn, the Pilgrims, who did not call themselves Pilgrims, but Saints, came over as Protestant Separatists who sought a "New World." I find it fascinating to read such history over and again of those who sought a new world for the sake of religious freedom, specifically a greater form of Christian liberty, and that America was the destination for their new world of life, liberty and revolutionary faith.

They came to build a new government of church and state, where both would support and empower their freedom to actually live their faith in daily life. *And live it they would.* They helped set the stage for the American forefathers of the Revolution to fight for their faith, a fight that we now face in culture like never before.

Church & State

It was interesting to me while running for Congress those around the community who would comment on social media posts negatively, telling me to keep my faith out of politics. The ironic thing, to me, was that I hadn't even mentioned my faith as a principle to legislate; they actually brought it up before I did.

The truth of the matter is that I wouldn't want to legislate my faith. I want legislation that continues the framework of the early pioneers of our nation, but that is a framework of freedom, not religion. I want the freedom to live my faith out loud, to freely give life to others and to culture in a positive way because of my faith. I do not however want it legislated on others. That would take away the power of freedom, and you can't have genuine change or transformation apart from freedom of choice—as long as those choices don't directly infringe upon another. And let's be clear, there is a vast difference between actual infringement and the more common reaction of taking offense that permeates our culture today.

Let me give you an example of the power of choice in our faith apart from legislation. This may sound funny so please don't misinterpret me here, but I don't want prayer legislated back in schools. I don't want the Bible mandated in schools. I do however want the freedom for both to be *allowed* in schools, and for my kids not to have other religions, beliefs or supposed cultural norms forced upon them.

I want kids praying in school because they *want* to, not because they *have* to. I want kids bringing their Bible to school because they live off of it, not just because it's an assignment in a class. In fact, if you look at the examples of persecution for faith in cultures or nations around the world you will find that when something wasn't allowed, it caused the true fire to burn small but authentic and strong at first. When something is taken away, you'll find a remnant that rise up to bring it to life in grassroots fashion. Now, I am not in any way advocating for disallowing of prayer or the Word, I don't want it legislated for or against. I just want freedom for people to get passionate, to start their own slow, hot burn out of a lukewarm state so as to inspire others to do the same.

I'll never forget holding prayer meetings during high school; whether at church, at school, at home, in parks, you name it! But prayer was never coordinated or forced upon any of those meetings or classrooms. I loved carrying my beat up, worn out Bible with me so I could feast off it throughout the day, or just have it as my foundation on my person. Yet, I never had a Bible class in my school that gave me required reading. Still, the fire grew stronger.

This is what a government of hope is all about; it is an uprising of passion, of hearts yielded to a King whose government they—*we*—get to bring about here on earth as it is in heaven. I don't want legislation to do my job or purpose for me, that's what God calls *us* to do. He calls us to be that government. He calls us to use our freedoms that our government leaders and legislation do give us so that we can be who God created us to be.

One of the greatest marks of William Penn's life was the religious liberty he went after with his whole heart. Why? He didn't do so because he was fighting to legislate something, he did so because he wanted the freedom to truly *live* something.

Our New World

"Enlarge the place of your tent, and let them stretch out the curtains of your dwellings; do not spare; lengthen your cords, and strengthen your stakes. For you shall expand to the right and to the left, and your descendants will inherit the nations, and make the desolate cities inhabited." (Isaiah 54:2-3)

I want to use the rest of this book to propose a general outline (with some applicable strategies & blueprints) for our own "Mayflower Compact." If we want to cross over into the new world we've been praying for, here on earth as it is in heaven, now is the time! We have a government in office that has continued to fight for the religious liberty that was established by the Pilgrims/Saints when they crossed over, by William Penn when he crossed over, and by our Revolutionary Forefathers when they came and established America as the United States.

We need to take advantage of this time in history when the waters are being held back on our behalf; but they aren't there to do the job for us. We the people are the ones who must seize the moment of a new era, and we must do so far beyond our vote—and our services. We must stand up and use our freedom wisely, courageously and informally.

In his book, "*Dreaming with God*," Pastor Bill Johnson once wrote about a lesson he learned from the Lord: *"What comes into the house must have a way out of the house, or it will die in the house."* The "house" that is the church, believers, the Body of Christ, must like never before use every bit of freedom we have been given, or else that freedom will die under-utilized.

If we don't want an unjust government forced upon us, than we must rise up and live out, together, the very government that Jesus carried into this world on His shoulders. We must take the freedom we have now to stand up from our familiar and expected comforts, leave our dependence upon the pots of meat Egypt gives to us, cross over the tumultuous waters we feel raging against us and establish this new world ALL AROUND us.

It is our time, our *kairos*—our moment—to *be* a government of hope for the world, before all that we're left with is a government that takes that hope away. Keep voting for good leaders, keep praying for them, and I hope we will keep in office those who will continue to hold back the waters of oppression. But we cannot depend on them to live our purpose for us. We need to realize that like on the Mayflower, we are arriving upon a New World, perhaps different than we would have expected. And we need to have a plan of how we mobilize a government of hope that is God-dependent, rather than man-dependent.

"You may choose to look the other way but you can never say again that you did not know." - William Wilberforce

"Arise, shine; for your light has come! And the glory of the Lord is risen upon you. For behold, the darkness shall cover the earth, and deep darkness the people; But the Lord will arise over you, and His glory will be seen upon you." (Isaiah 60:1-2)

Chapter 4:

The Blueprint: A Family Structure

"Unless the Lord builds the house, they labor in vain who build it..." (Psalm 127:1)

One of the driving reasons we ran for U.S. House of Representatives is because of what we believe the "House" or society of our nation is supposed to be all about. Unfortunately, much of that house is constructed as a political and power structure which has leaked in and infected so many other parts of culture that steer us towards platform-based influence and the valuing of tangible measurements over intangible fruit.

To me, the role of a representative in the U.S. House, or any leader in any house for that matter, is supposed to be that of a servant leader, one who serves and empowers others from the bottom, up. This posture doesn't position us for gain as readily, but it will posture us for further-reaching and longer-lasting forms of multiplication that echo through society beyond our control.

We don't need to go far into it here to all know how the power and political structures in place have created the corruption that many of us are looking, hoping, praying and acting upon to see changed. We don't need to go into the details of the political manipulation for power, or for how this type of structure has made us so "ladder-focused." What we do need to address is our opportunity to shift our cultural mindset from prioritizing one kind of structure over another.

When my dad first got into ministry, he left behind a very successful and rising T.V. news anchor career in Fresno, CA. He waffled and prayed for some time over this life-changing shift. It wasn't until one Sunday morning listening to the Pastor offer the following words that he knew he himself had to make such a shift. The Pastor looked out at the congregation and my dad felt as if he zeroed in on him directly when he said: "You can climb the ladder of success your whole life only to find that it has been propped against the wrong building."

My mom, still holding my dad's hand and praying during this whole exchange squeezed his hand gently as tears began to trickle down his face. She whispered quietly, *You have your answer, don't you.* And he did. My dad and mom went forward in ministry and missions that would impact many across the nations, perhaps millions through the ensuing multiplication. And it all happened because one life shifted its investment, moving the ladder of success from one structure to another.

With the division and discord in politics and its tug-o-war over society, here is a similar shift we are ripe for in all of culture. Perhaps politicians won't initiate it for us, but we can make sure that this shift begins in our churches, businesses, organizations, cities, communities, cultures and the like.

We can take our "ladders" of aspiration and use them to serve others, to flip our culture's natural top-down power structures into one that truly empowers people and leaders— new, emerging leaders—from the bottom, up. We can make our ladders into vehicles that serve others and all of society, rather than have them only serve ourselves.

Many individuals and corporate bodies have already made such a shift on a micro level, concerning their own interests and how they see and do. What we are proposing is for us to build this type of structure on a macro level, one revolutionary life at a time and interwoven across our communities, *together*.

Again, most of the nation's top leaders probably won't lead this change for us. And truth be told such reformation is sometimes better through free, grassroots stimulation than it is through legislation, but we'll discuss that more later.

So, it is we who have to make the change by removing our ladder from the building we've too long been focused on. These structures we've climbed have often been, unknowingly, re-enforced by political and power structures that are familiar and built into our plans. What if we give our attention instead to the "Family Structure" that matches the blueprint our Everlasting Father has been building since the beginning of time? It's the blueprint that I believe the needy and broken parts of our culture are crying out for today, and we have it right in our back pocket. All it requires is a shift in our perspective to see the bigger picture through God's lens of *family*.

The House of David

> **"Also the Lord tells you that He will make you a house." (2 Samuel 7:11)**

This has become one of the most formative promises in my life. Will I cease from what I am building to recognize what God is, and has been building? It's easy to say yes, but often our good intentions lead us to believe that the good work we are doing in a micro perspective must automatically match up with what God is doing from a macro perspective. What if we have the right idea, but that idea is still being influenced by or conformed to known structures or methods of the status quo? What if we have the correct "Major" and "Minor" in theory, just the wrong order of priority? What if God is waiting for us to take what we have learned in our individual projects, and give it freely to building His special, societal, *governmental*, family project?

I personally received this directive word from 2 Samuel 7:11 shortly after my wife, our daughter Mercy, and I had moved to Addis Ababa, Ethiopia in 2008. We started mentoring a young man, Alex, who had grown up on the poorest of streets and living in a plastic house on his own. He had just gotten out of prison, a charge that had come by wrong association, and he was ready for a new start. God showed us the light and potential in Alex that was so contrary to his circumstances. And God used Alex (in many ways) to deliver this timely word to us to remind us what God actually had in store for us in Ethiopia.

Alex and I had begun meeting to go through a prayer curriculum I had written, and I was teaching him how to get quiet and listen to the Lord's voice. It had only been a few days when Alex showed up at our doorstep unannounced and said, *"Uhhh, I think I have a word for you."* A little stunned at first, because I'm not sure Alex even knew what "having a word" meant, but Alex had been practicing his time of waiting on God when he was directed to this verse, the same words God gave David, but for us.

We had moved to Ethiopia in early 2008 to partner with local leaders and open a large empowerment center to help local young people come out of poverty and make an impact in the world. We had gone as far as having architectural and land blueprints professionally drawn up. We had the right intentions, I believe, and even the right method of empowering youth and those in the margins, but we were trying to build all this through an old structure.

See, when God gave this word to David it was because David as you probably know wanted to build God a house. David wanted to build a place to house God's presence, to worship, a place for intimacy with the Lord. David had the purest motives possible for wanting to build God a house. And still, God told David, *"No, I will make you a house."*

The word house here has two very different, definitive constructs. The first and most obvious definition is that of a *"physical structure,"* which could be a building, a temple/church, a home, etc. The second meaning for the word house is that of a *"family structure,"* which is a family, a lineage of descendants, clan, or a heritage. What we find is that David wanted to build God a *physical structure*, but God was trying to make David into a *family structure*.

We are often doing all the right things for all the right reasons, but in the midst of such, little do we know we are still operating off of the world's typical blueprints; building first and foremost through physical structures. All the while, God has been and still is trying to build a family structure in, with and through our lives.

This is the shift in overall model that we have to make, and when we do we will find that so much of what we have already been building so beautifully will become even more fruitful and will construct something of a new and reformed world around us with exponential change, right in the midst of the chaos we are currently so frustrated by. We can watch struggle become strength.

God's Blueprint for Family

God has been building this type of family structure from the beginning of time. He first established the institution of family as a governing agent of life and change in the Garden, where Adam and Eve's first purpose in order to build and subdue the earth was to be fruitful and multiply. During the flood, God saved a remnant of humanity through the family of Noah. Then, God re-started His family blueprint intended to cover the nations through Abraham, whose promise wasn't tower's, temple's or teachings but that he would be a *father of nations*, and his seed would be greater than the stars in the sky or the sand on the seashore.

It was through Abraham's grandson, Jacob, that God established the institution of government, by transforming Jacob from the inside-out and renaming him Israel. It was Jacob's sons that would become the twelve governing tribes of Israel. Again, God established this government through an identity shift and a family structure.

The list goes on and on throughout scripture. Before David was the man or "house" we have discussed, the man we know as the "Kinsman" or "Family Redeemer," Boaz, changed the course of history through what in the moment could feel like the smallest of actions. But Boaz' astounding love and care for Ruth birthed a child, named Obed. Obed also had a son, named Jesse. And Jesse too had a son, bringing us back to David, who God made into a house, a lineage of descendants that birthed the promised Son, Jesus.

Then Jesus, both the Son of God and Son of Man, died and rose again, tore down the old "house" and rebuilt it in three days so that we could all be adopted into the family, not just slaves or servants, *but sons and daughters*. And when Jesus ascended into Heaven He did as He promised He would by sending a Helper, the Spirit of Adoption as He was called, Who we more typically refer to as the Holy Spirit. At that point, the Spirit came down upon them in the books of Acts and the apostles formed the early Church as we know it, the third institution that God established which once again was birthed through God's unending, persevering lens of a family structure.

And here we are today, the church, a body of believers still working to build His kingdom like David wanted, through physical structures that are more outwardly tangible and therefore more rewarding in the moment for us. And still, our Everlasting Father endures with us, consistently working, weaving and making all things work together for the good—woven into the blueprint He has been focused on the entire time—*The Family Structure.*

In Day 2 of my book, "If God Had A House," I wrote about a time in history when God was calling His people to make just this sort of change, telling them to "*get to work*" in building His true house rather than their own:

"In the first year of King Cyrus, King Cyrus issued a decree concerning the house of God...Let the house be rebuilt..." (Ezra 6:3)

Almost seven years ago I had an experience with the Lord that I will never forget. I woke up in our then home in Ethiopia, stood out up out of bed and couldn't stop speaking out, 'Ezra 6, Ezra 6, Ezra 6.' The only way I could describe the experience was as if a burning coal had branded the words on my lips before I got up. I hadn't looked at the book of Ezra in years, and never had I made it a personal point of focus.

After this experience I dove in and kept searching for what the Lord was speaking to me, or perhaps even through me. One of the primary passages the Lord led me to through its close connection to Ezra 6 was Haggai 2—a chapter that, like the passage above, is also specifically geared towards the rebuilding of God's house.

"So get to work, Zerubbabel!' God is speaking. 'Get to work, Joshua son of Jehozadak—high priest!' 'Get to work, all you people!'—God is speaking. 'Yes, get to work! For I am with you' The God-of-the-Angel-Armies is speaking!'

'This what God-of-the-Angel-Armies said: 'Before you know it, I will shake up sky and earth, ocean and fields. And I'll shake down all the godless nations. They'll bring bushels of wealth and I will fill this Temple with splendor.' God-of-the-Angel-Armies says so.

'I own the silver. I own the gold,' Decree of God-of-the-Angel-Armies. 'This temple is going to end up far better than it started out, a glorious beginning but an even more glorious finish: a place in which I will hand out wholeness and holiness.' Decree of God-of-the-Angel-Armies." (Haggai 2:4-9, The Message)

Ezra, Zerubbabel, and Joshua son of Jehozadak were each key figures during this special window of opportunity to rebuild God's house. However, it was not only a message to these who represented the Government and the Church leaders, but God addressed 'all you people' when He commanded them to 'Get to work' on the rebuilding of His house."

Shifting Our Priorities

Truly, for most of us it is only a shift, a re-prioritization, and then it's learning to live it out intentionally across society together. We've probably known about the people or multiplication-focused element of this family structure concept as it could be stated that it is just like discipleship on a broader scale. Unfortunately, on a macro level it has too often remained our "Minor," or the bi-product of the physical and power structures we've "Majored" in, and therefore we haven't given it our greatest investment, *yet*.

The reality is that both are good, and needed, we just have to flip how we prioritize the two and which one becomes supportive of the other. The family structure must be our blueprint, and the physical structures then naturally become supportive pillars to keep building through and around.

My favorite example of this is in regards to a faith-based or humanitarian mission. Typically we embark on such missions to very impoverished areas with the agenda of building a house or a church. Let me say that this is an incredible and needed gift, one that my family and I have been part of multiple times as well. But what I find most telling is that these building projects are the "Major" focus of our teams and trips. Yet after we leave and return home to daily life, we usually find that the greatest impact of the trip came from the bi-product of what we were building for the people; we find that what left the biggest mark on our soul are the connections we made with some of the locals, whose names, faces and their joy amid their poverty will be emblazoned on our hearts forever.

And I dare say that after our trip, if we were to ask the people that we built these homes and churches for, that they, too, would say the most memorable takeaway won't be the tangible building in front of them, but the time you put your arm around them, connected with them, valued them, and made them feel part of a family that was beyond their circumstances—like they *belonged*.

So, the two greatest points of impact on our trips are usually the intangible, people-oriented moments that were actually only the bi-products of our intended plan, which was to build them a house. If we have that much fruit without it even being our most prioritized investment, how much more fruit would there be if we made that area our priority of investment? Both are necessary. One is incredibly needed and useful, and the other is life-changing and multiplying.

We naturally tend to rely too heavily upon our physical structures, even if that's not always our intent. What will happen when we begin to set out with the agenda of building a family structure more consistently? We will build *through* people even more than we build for them. Our results won't be as momentary, but in the long run they will be exponential to serve and disciple cities, cultures, and nations.

On the Streets

After Alex gave us that word originally meant for David, we took our vision and investment out of a building project for the youth and marginalized in Addis Ababa and put our focus fully on empowering the people into a family structure throughout the streets. Instead of building a property, a church, an organization or programs within a structure, we sought to see reformation across a city.

We have so many stories from that time that simply blew us away. We watched Alex change from one with potential who was barely hanging on in life into someone street kids all through the streets followed and thought of as a father. More emerging leaders like Alex started to build this way with us. Soon we had shelters and programs to help hold up and support the intangible structure that was developing. We saw these small groups of youth in one of the capitals of the world's poverty begin to rise up out of their circumstances and become leaders who impacted their families and communities.

We didn't personally build something lasting that we can point to as ours. But we saw a greater, societal family come from the ashes in a way that kept going long after we left. It was *beyond us*, beyond our measurements, beyond our buildings, and beyond our results. See, in a family structure it's not necessarily about "our," it's about the bigger picture of transformation.

We never got the amazing blueprint or property we had dreamed of. God had different designs on what He was making us into. And before we knew it, we had a family structure that spanned the streets. We had young leaders like Alex who became fathers and mothers across the community. They were the ones the youth or their families (if they had one) would come to for help and a way forward. Many of the kids on the streets of Addis came from down country, rural areas that were oppressed by poverty. They ran from home to try and find hope in the city. Instead they started living on the streets and poverty had overtaken them.

That's when God gave us a strategy, an upside down strategy to see that hope realized. See, usually we operate from those top-down power structures to create influence—and this can be a powerful way to release such new strategies as well. But the Lord showed us a bottom-up strategy that we'll get into far more in the next chapter.

The reality of it was simple, though—*every life had something to give*. No matter how young or how bound by poverty or addiction, every life could multiply to others. And that is where a family structure begins.

Chapter 5:

The Socioeconomic Entry Point

"For you know the grace of our Lord Jesus Christ, that though He was rich, yet for your sake He became poor, that you through His poverty might become rich." (2 Corinthians 8:9)

"A team is only as strong as its weakest link." I believe the same is true for a family, a business, and the society of a nation. But do we really adhere to this old adage?

What if we did? What if we actually built the house of our nation—the family that America, or any nation, once was—not from a top-down power structure, but from a bottom-up form of empowerment? What if we invested in the "weakest link" the same way we do a CEO or an "influencer" with a platform? What if we holistically invested in people the way Jesus did?

What if we gave people value and worth, not just money? What if we gave them belonging, not just survival? What if we gave them our time and talents so as to extract the vision and purpose that's hidden inside of them? What if we put people before politics, before profits, before programs or agenda and built through them by consistently empowering them with

---

greater opportunity? What if we shared our ladder with others as a bridge over poverty, brokenness and lack, as a means to go out to the world in their purpose—not just a way for us or them to go up?

Let me be clear, this is not a "share the pot" system to divide wealth and create dependence, but a plan to give belonging, vision, purpose and worth to those who are struggling to flourish. This is an exercise of our free market which will actually fortify our freedom, but it requires a perspective and a measure of servant leadership. Through such, we can take the strengths of our capitalism and actually multiply those strengths by empowering those in a state of economic "weakness." This will build the foundation of our house and see the investment not go down through the drain of poverty but be recycled back up through the rest of culture over time.

Perhaps you have seen the illustration of the pack of wolves walking through a snowy wilderness. The pack travels in a line, but it's the most vulnerable who are out in front, setting the pace. The five strongest wolves follow next, protecting them from attack. Then you have a stable, fully protected group in the middle; they precede the next five strongest wolves that help strengthen and protect the pack from behind. And finally, in the back we find the leader—the one with the most influence. The lead wolf is not out in front but is serving, caring and leading the whole pack from behind—*strengthening everyone from this position!*

This is what a "Family Structure" looks like. When we take the model for family and apply it to our perspective and plans of *how* we build society, we'll see our "house" transformed.

This breaks down into and demonstrates for us a socioeconomic model of how we build our house, family or nation from the bottom, up. For leaders or those with the most influence it is not about being in power, but using such a position or influence to empower others. That becomes true for us all—how are we using our ladders? How will we use our influence to flip the power structure into a family structure and empower people forward, and onward? When we learn to invest differently in the foundational layers of a family structure, the layers that are usually entrapped by the greatest struggles of society, we will be rewarded over time by seeing the foundation of the whole house raised up, and the investment we place there will actually be recycled upward and strengthen the house in its entirety.

Society's Foundation

If we are truly only as strong as our weakest link, that would mean that the greatest struggles or issues of our culture and community are not just weeds that need to be taken care of for appearance sake but they are actually the foundation of our society. Yet, whether through our welfare system or other cultural mindsets, these areas of poverty and brokenness are merely given a band-aid for an internal wound and treated to survive in society and too rarely seen for who they are, restored in their worth, *empowered*, built upon, and actually built through.

> **"'Can anything good come out of Nazareth?' Phillip said to him. '*Come and see.*'" (John 1:46, emphasis mine.)**

These foundational "issues" such as poverty, substance abuse, immigration and refugees, foster and orphan care, trafficking, the criminal justice system and more affect us all. In our current model, no matter what "higher than the bottom" social class we are in, we will continue to watch people we know and a culture that surrounds us fall downward into the issues below us. And they will continue to do so until we truly believe that these "issues" are foundational people who can and will change our society, if we will invest in and empower them in a new way.

Currently, our welfare system is broken and the calls for socialism are getting louder. Why? Our freedom has largely become selfish. We have forgotten how to use our freedom corporately, and if we don't use it freely to benefit the whole house, it will be taken from us, divided among us, and we'll all slide downward without hope instead of *everyone* rising up together. We absolutely can see the struggles of our society become strengths and the foundation for a new kind of growth, as well as a new kind of hope for us all.

That is how, and to whom Jesus imparted hope at every turn. His most triumphal entry would confound every strategy the world's greatest leaders might ever come up with. Jesus had His followers retrieve a chosen donkey for Him to ride into His victory upon. He chose a donkey as the point of entry to fulfill the government He was, and is, establishing. *Will we recognize that donkey, that unlikely entry point for change, today?*

> **"Go into the village opposite you, and immediately you will find a donkey tied, and a colt with her. Loose them and bring them to Me. And if anyone says anything to you, you shall say, 'The Lord has need of them,' and immediately he will send them...**
>
> *'Behold, your King is coming to you,*
> *Lowly, and sitting on a donkey.'"*
> **(Matthew 21:2-3, 5)**

Re-building society in this way by seeing our "issues" as a foundation an opportunity requires a renewed perspective from us all. Our perspective is a limit or a fire hose on what naturally and freely flows out of our life. We have to re-focus in order to re-allocate. We have to see people not through the dependence-model they've been fed from but according to who they were created to be in God's image; see the strengths, not just the struggle.

We have to imagine what could come out of them, if empowered in such a way. It will change not just the amount, but the *nature* of our giving. Investment is very different than giving. And we only invest in things or people that we believe in. So we will not and cannot flip these foundational issues in our culture unless we start to see people that we believe in, even when it seems to be counter-intuitive at first glance.

The Empty Vessels

We began on this strategic journey of transformation through empowering the powerless when God gave us a specific word a few years before we moved to Ethiopia. In fact, this word helped pinpoint our move to Ethiopia before the "Family Structure" directive and we've found that it is the key to rebuilding a true family structure across a city, culture or nation.

I lied on the bed in prayer in our apartment in Fresno, CA unsure of our next steps, and without provision to take them. We had vision and calling from the Lord that burned in our hearts, but how to see it come about amid our current circumstances? We didn't know where to begin. I asked the Lord for a fresh word from Him, and after a few minutes, once prompted I flipped open my Bible and landed on this passage that forever changed our family, and thankfully, many other families as well:

> "A certain woman of the wives of the sons of the prophets cried out to Elisha, saying, 'Your servant my husband is dead, and you know that your servant feared the LORD. And the creditor is coming to take my two sons to be his slaves.'
>
> So Elisha said to her, 'What shall I do for you? Tell me, what do you have in the house?' And she said, 'Your maidservant has nothing in the house but a jar of oil.' Then he said, 'Go, borrow vessels from everywhere, from all your neighbors—empty vessels; do not gather just a few. And when you have come in, you shall shut the door behind you and your sons; then pour it into all those vessels, and set aside the full ones.'
>
> So she went from him and shut the door behind her and her sons, who brought *the vessels* to her; and she poured it out.
>
> Now it came to pass, when the vessels were full, that she said to her son, 'Bring me another vessel.' And he said to her, 'There is not another vessel.' So the oil ceased.
>
> Then she came and told the man of God. And he said, 'Go, sell the oil and pay your debt; and you and your sons live on the rest.'" **(2 Kings 4:1-7)**

The empty vessels are a picture of how we can see our cities, our culture and even a nation transformed. The empty vessels are the beginning of a strategy to see how our corporate struggles can be turned into strengths. The empty vessels are a picture of an unlikely approach to stimulate our economy, and what is more, to stimulate the value and purpose of people to be redeemed from bondage and empowered to be one who has something to give; because truly, *we all have something to give.*

Here we had a woman who was in poverty, and she was about to lose her children into debt and bondage. Elisha asked her such an interesting question, *"What do you have in your house?"* It reminds me of the same question I grew up hearing my mom ask, and her mom, and her mom before that; *"What do you have in your hands?"* What's so interesting, and culturally on point for us as well is the woman's response, *"I have nothing but a jar of oil."*

In the same sentence she said both that she had nothing, and that she had a jar of oil. Essentially, she was calling her oil "nothing." I think we all can do that fairly often, especially when we have some form of lack or need. We tend to focus on what we don't have, rather than creative ways to utilize what we do have. And when given or spent in the right way, God is a specialist at multiplying our "nothing" into more than enough.

Look at Elisha's next directive to her, once she mentions her oil. "Go and gather empty vessels..." And that is the exact directive the Lord gave us as a strategy of reformation and revival. God wanted us to see what He could do through an empty vessel, because not only are there many of such vessels across our cultures and communities, but Jesus prioritizes them and often does miracles through them.

As mentioned when we began this journey towards a government of hope, God has a knack for using the foolish to confound the wise, the weak to confound the strong, and the base things to bring to nothing the things that are elevated. So to send us, or the woman in the story, to gather *empty* vessels may seem like a counter-intuitive way to accumulate worth or pay off debt; in God's government of hope, it's the exact way He usually brings the greatest stories of redemption and reformation.

If we will each learn to take what we have in our hands, whether that is our time, our talents, our treasures or the like, and pour them out freely into the empty vessels of our culture and society, we might just find that the oil keeps multiplying until there are no more empty vessels to speak of until debt is paid off, bondage is broken and we all get to go forward, to keep living and thriving off the rest.

The empty vessels are an unlikely but vital entry point for the increase of the government of hope that Jesus carried in on His shoulders. If we will gather said empty vessels, *believe in them*, and empower them with what we have to give, we too will see a multiplication in the very place we fear there will be lack. Our family knows this from experience, as we set out to search the world for empty vessels. And that's how God planted us in Ethiopia. We saw this strategy come alive and through it formed the family structure that our culture desperately needs.

Finding Neverland

To be honest, it took us a little while to break free from the typical structures of how to do ministry, how to bring change, etc. We began this mandate right away, or so we thought. But we were still going to the "full vessels" of society, people or leaders of influence, to help start this strategy. And we kept striking out. We had to adjust the structure we believed and invested in and find a way to go straight to the empty vessels. It took a special movie to help figure this out.

The movie, *Finding Neverland*, is about the story of the playwright James Barrie, the creator of Peter Pan. He had already had a very successful career in London, but his recent work was falling on deaf ears, it had seemed he lost his touch. But one day Mr. Barrie began spending time with a widow and her young boys. He got out of his "adult" world and mindsets long enough to dream again, and believe. Before he knew it, he was authoring a new play about pirates, fairies, and pixie dust and creating this imaginative childlike world. He went to the proprietor of the theatre that housed his plays and began to share eagerly about his new work.

The proprietor looked at James and essentially said, "What self-respecting doctor, lawyer or businessman of high-society London is going to watch a play about pirates, fairies, flying and the like?" James nodded, seemingly understanding his point of view. So he told the proprietor, "On opening night, I need you to save me twenty-five seats scattered across the auditorium."

The proprietor jumped back in with the typical questions, wondering aloud, "Who are in these seats? Are they paid for?" To which Mr. Barrie, in so many words, replied: "Just save me twenty-five seats that are scattered about, I'll take care of the rest."

The cast scoffed at much of this childlike set, their costumes and the premise of this wild tale. But opening night came despite their doubts and they were approaching the curtain call. The twenty-five seats still sat empty, James Barrie and others getting nervous and restless among the otherwise packed house of high society London. Just then, right before the play was to begin a group of twenty-five orphans ran up to the theatre and they were taken to the seats that were saved and scattered for them.

The story of Peter Pan began for the very first time. But as it began, just as the proprietor feared, the people who made up that class of London just didn't "get it." They couldn't connect with the uniquely special ride Mr. Barrie had created for them. Silence and discomfort covered the auditorium.

But then something happened; the orphaned children or "empty vessels" of society who should never have had a seat in an uptown play began to laugh. They got it. They understood. They weren't too full of themselves or the world's "adult" ways and therefore they had room enough to receive it all—*and they loved it*!

Before you knew it the kids' laughter and enjoyment was contagious. One by one the adults started to return to their own childlike roots and roars of laughter and joy filled the theatre. But it started with the unlikely ones who shouldn't have been there. It began with the empty vessels, and then it multiplied up through the "adults" of society who would have thought such to be beneath them, or counter intuitive to how things should be done.

That was the beginning of the now world renown story of *Peter Pan*. It is a reminder that, sometimes, full vessels aren't the place to start because they are full of the old ways; the typical, the expected, and to be honest, often just full of self. But that's just the thing about those who are empty, they aren't so full of the status quo and they have room to receive the new blessings God wants to pour out.

"A satisfied soul loathes the honeycomb, but to a hungry soul every bitter thing is sweet." (Proverbs 27:7)

Empowering the Powerless

One of the biggest keys to this whole empty-vessel, family-structure blueprint is that it is built through empowerment; not through the typical forms of dependence that are so prevalent within systems of need. Most of the last fifteen years of my life, if not longer, have been spent on developing ways of empowering people to change a culture or a nation. One of the things we've found is that empowerment is not easy. It can be messy and not cut-and-dry at all. But if we stick through it with people it is always worth it.

First, I want to share with you one specific story that helped affirm and reform our own understanding of why empowerment is so vital to re-building people, culture, and society as a whole. Then, we'll share some of how that empowerment came to life in and through some of those most unlikely vessels in Ethiopia.

There is a cultural practice when eating Ethiopian food called *gousha*. Typically, when enjoying Ethiopian cuisine you eat with your hands, using pieces of a spongy, pancake like staple, called *injera*, to pick up bites of meat, lentils, sauces, veggies and things of that sort. To *gousha* someone is to do exactly that, but instead of picking up a bite and feeding yourself, you reach across and feed the bite in your hand to someone else. I have to admit, my first experiences with this were unexpected and a little uncomfortable, until someone explained why they were putting their hand in our mouths, of course.

One thing we used to like to do with some of the groups of kids from the street we worked with was to take them out to lunch at a local café. Often times, there would be a handful of the kids who hadn't eaten that day, or perhaps longer. Some might say they were the picture of poverty as the world knows it. But these kids were becoming like family to us, and something amazing started to take place at these meals.

The kids were thrilled to be out at a café, and very thankful for the opportunity to have a good meal, but it was the camaraderie we all shared that was most memorable. Before we knew it, the kids began taking turns to *gousha* us. At first we didn't think anything of it until we realized that here were kids with nothing in their belly, probably not knowing where their next meal is coming from, and their greatest joy wasn't feeding themselves. Rather, their greatest joy was when we allowed them to feed us.

Think about that again for a minute. It can mess with our rationale of how to address poverty when the most hungry get fed at a deeper level when they are the ones feeding you. The truth is that this revelation fit right in with the concepts of empowerment God had us focused on with those in the streets.

We would always do our best to take care of their physical needs, of anywhere between about 20 to 75 kids during a season. But those physical acts of welfare would usually go right back down the drain of dependence, if not attached to some forward path; they needed something to stick to. That's where we found that the greatest difference was made when we empowered the locals in need with three different more intangible things:

1. *Belonging, or family.*
2. *Vision, or purpose.*
3. *Value and worth.*

Belonging/Family

This is one part of why the kids loved to *gousha* us so much, because to let someone stick their hand in your mouth to feed you, especially someone coming from these kids' external circumstances, shows them an unspoken form of love and acceptance. Sure, there were nervous moments for us because most of them had dirty, cut up, snotty hands most of the time. They would wash them before meals, but the dynamic was still there. It let them feel like part of a family, like there wasn't so much separation as economic-driven social classes try to articulate.

This is the same premise we mentioned as being vital to building a family structure, putting emphasis on connection with people before agenda. It means something to them. Many in poverty feel so much shame and condemnation that usually our quality time is worth far more than any amount of money.

Vision/Purpose

Typically we reserve things like "vision" for CEO's or entrepreneurs. But there is a reason the book of Proverbs reminds us that **"without vision, the people perish." (Proverbs 29:18)**

It's a mental/emotional staple, because it creates self-motivation, self-accountability, and overall hope. Those are principles we usually try to teach people to use to overcome addiction or poverty. But if you can help them find vision, most people will suddenly become a lot more self-motivated and accountable. We don't have to draw as many boundaries for people if we give them a hopeful vision to run for. It's part of flipping our power structure so that vision isn't reserved for those in the boardroom, but it is cultivated among the broken so that they can see forward in a new way.

If someone in poverty uses only their natural sight to see themselves, they may look at their hands and say, "I have nothing." But if you give them vision, you give them permission to look beyond their circumstances and see the innate purpose, gifts, talents and hope they were created with inside. Those things were always there; we just don't spend enough time helping those at the bottom to realize that they have just as much purpose as we do.

Value/Worth

This one traces right back to the *gousha* analogy. Essentially, you help them become a giver, and in doing so you help prove their already-existing worth. Otherwise, we go about poverty care or the various difficult issues of society and as they fight off shame and condemnation we continue to tell them, "You have worth, you have value." But then our actions always make them a recipient, virtually disproving their worth. When we help them become a giver right off the bat, we help them take their eyes off of themselves, off their circumstances and needs, off their dependence, and with that one small action we help prove their value by helping them realize they really do have something to give—they have purpose within a bigger family.

Alex's Next Steps

Shortly after moving to Ethiopia we felt a prompting from the Lord to invite Alex to come and live with us. We had been learning to walk the streets with him and at the same time showing him how to love those he encountered on the streets like Jesus would. After just a couple days living with us Alex quickly realized that we did not live like most foreigners he had been around, particularly in finances where we were genuinely trusting God each day for when, how and where funds would come from. Alex became part of this daily faith walk with us.

One day, with about $250 cash to left to live off of, brand new to a new part of the world, we felt God prompting us to do something radical. We felt led to take all the money we had left and give it to Alex. Now, this was a little concerning on two different fronts. First, we didn't know where our next provision would come from to pay for food, bills, etc.

Second, Alex had grown up in a very dependence oriented kind of poverty and we were worried what a sudden influx of cash all at once like this could do to him, we didn't want it to cause a setback for his growth. However, we kept feeling this prompting from the Lord so we said, "Yes."

I'll never forget that night that Destiny and I walked into the kitchen where we had asked Alex to meet us. We took all of our cash, put it in his hands, and simply said, "God wants you to have it." And we encouraged him to ask the Lord how He would have him use it, but the decision would be up to him.

What Alex did with that money was life-changing. Instead of it breaking him in a bad way, he was so overwhelmed to be trusted in that way, by God and by us, that he prayed over every bill he used or handed out. He went to the bank and had it broken down into small bills which he carried around with him on the streets that we had been walking together.

He started investing in the people on the streets, especially kids—taking them out for tea or lunch—or buying them a shoeshine box to give them work. He only spent a small fraction of the money on himself, and then he came home one day with his hands full of groceries for all of us as a family to eat off of until God provided again.

When we looked back over all God did to build a family structure in those streets of Addis Ababa, Ethiopia, a lot of it could be traced back to that $250 that Alex started planting like seeds in the lowliest places of the community. Before we knew it, those seeds started to bloom through people and a great multiplication was formed through that one act of unbridled empowerment.

Unlikely Leaders

When we began to work with orphans and street kids in Ethiopia, our belief was that if we invested those three things we mentioned previously; Belonging, Vision, and Value, that despite their circumstances we could see them become leaders and contributing members of society even at young age.

First, we began with a group of eight kids in an orphanage or children's home. We spent one full day with them per week, mostly giving them love and our belief. We spoke to them in ways that would empower them, we created opportunities for them to step up and have something to give.

I'll never forget one weekend when we had them all over to our house to spend two nights for something of a retreat. We talked to them more about God's purpose for their lives. These were 9 to 14 year old kids, mind you, and we challenged them to think and pray about God's perspective of the kids on the streets, who had even less care or opportunity than what these eight orphans had.

We gave each of the eight kids a piece of paper and a pen and sent them off around our home and compound to spend some time with God, pray, and ask Him what He would want to say to the kids on the streets. After an hour or so we came back together in our living room where I had set up a white board.

Now, I love brainstorming and dreaming sessions, and have had many of them with other leaders, groups, etc. But nothing matched this white board session with those the world would call orphans. To listen to the ideas they had, to hear what they felt God wanted to say to the other kids on the streets, was astounding. I was blown away.

In fact, we compiled many of their responses into resources in the local language and Alex and our team of spiritual fathers and mothers used them throughout the streets in their mentoring. So many kids who were living on the streets came into the "family" of God, and started to be empowered through such a family structure because of what those eight kids wrote. And then, the kids on the streets started to reach out to other kids like them. They started coming up with their own ideas. They started impacting their own families who were also living in forms of brokenness and poverty.

We watched an upward trajectory of multiplication take place through eight kids that from all outward, circumstantial appearances would be seen as nothing more than orphans who needed to be cared for. But they lived what we invested in them. And most of what we invested was the love of our time, and our belief. The value, the purpose, and the possibilities had all been inside them the whole time.

Most likely, those same things are waiting to be stimulated and extracted from within hundreds of thousands across our culture who are trapped in the things we see as bottom-of-society types of issues. We continue to send help down the lines of dependence to benefit their welfare. But what they really need is for you or I to believe in them a little more than what our money can do by itself and empower them to be and to live the purposeful, value-filled lives that they truly possess. If we will build *them*, they will re-build the foundation of our "house."

> "Jesus said to them, 'My food is to do the will of Him who sent Me, and to finish His work. Do you not say, 'There are still four months and the comes the harvest? Behold, I say to you, lift up your eyes and look at the fields, for they are already white for harvest!'" (John 4:34-35)

Jesus' Entry Point

> "For you know the grace of our Lord Jesus Christ, that though He was rich, yet for your sake He became poor, that you through His poverty might become rich." (2 Corinthians 8:9)

This verse can be a touchy subject. Not because we don't celebrate what Jesus did, but because we are often careful (for good reason) to subject ourselves to a mindset, life, or vow of poverty. And that is not at all what I am using it for. However, this verse is yet one more reason from our Lord's life and words why we cannot deny that Jesus made poverty His entry point for true change. It is another picture of why the King Jesus rode in to further establish His government on a donkey.

We are indeed called to be sons and daughters, and in and through Him we are called to rule and reign while establishing His kingdom here on earth as it is in heaven. But sometimes, we can get so caught up in living up to those parts of our identity that we forget the upside-down, servant nature of how He brought those truths to light for us all. And perhaps, that entry point is part of the path we are to follow when helping to empower others—all across society—to live like sons and daughters as well. No one builds a house from the roof, down. It always starts by excavating in the dirt and pouring a new mold to build upon.

Do you want to see reformation in your city, culture, or nation? Let's start with the empty vessels, and through them we may just uncover a living government of hope that is ready to multiply by what you pour through them.

Chapter 6:

The Real Thing

> "Now the multitude of those who believed were of one heart and one soul; neither did anyone say that any of the things he possessed was his own, but they had all things in common. And with great power the apostles gave witness to the resurrection of the Lord Jesus. And great grace was upon them all. Nor was there anyone among them who lacked..." (Acts 4:32-34)

If I've ever found the model for a government of hope lived out for us to see, here is a community that truly "got it." *They were in one heart and one soul. Great grace was upon them all. They gave witness with power. No one had any lack.* We've all read, heard or even used these phrases in reference to the astounding reality that took place there, but what is the necessary truth these apostles lived that provided life and change in a way that no earthly government ever could?

They operated in oneness, in freedom, in power, and with a spirit of generosity. And yet this passage from Acts 4 is merely a microcosm of the government of hope the early church lived out all throughout the book of Acts. Our biggest takeaway should be that with God, *it is possible*, and we all have a part to play in making it reality.

It is possible to be among a community that rises above what any other community has ever known. It is possible to defy reality. It is possible to come together in such a unity that exponential multiplication takes place. It is possible to overcome the selfish nature the world wants us to live through. It is possible to step beyond fear. It is possible to freely live and freely give the government that God has made available to us through Jesus. *It is possible...*

So many incredible testimonies came out of the book of Acts, and out of chapter 4 specifically. I've long believed it was a model for mission, and therefore a model for life. They literally began to live out the answer to Jesus' final prayer. And though they walked in power and healing to bring change, which I believe to be a most vital part of the hope we can, and should, bring to the world, there are two other main facets this early church lived out that are foundational to becoming this living blueprint.

These facets are unique and important to us living out an authentic government of hope, specifically versus the counterfeits that the world is trying to sneak in and replace them with. This community demonstrated an uncommon kind of *oneness*, and through such, together, they lived out a spirit of generosity that is and will be paramount to us bringing a government of hope into the world.

Here is a passage from my book, *The Power of Uncommon Unity*, from the chapter, *"A Kingdom Economy" (pgs. 127-128)*, discussing the testimony of Acts chapter 4 and the generation it is calling for *us* to be:

"The apostles who lived together as part of the answer to Jesus' final prayer lived in a unique community. It says they were of one heart and one soul. As was mentioned previously, this literally means to be 'in sync or in tune' with one another and to 'breathe spiritually together.' They lived together in a vitally powerful unity of community, and we learn that they themselves and the world around them were all the better for it. They walked in great grace and great power because of this uncommon unity. But what always strikes me is not just how they were united in Spirit, but also in the physical truths that were before them. In today's individualistic society, we welcome money, and it easily becomes our master. But within community, we can still appreciate money and resources; but here they become our servants to empower God's purposes and one another.

The word tells us that the believers 'had all things in common,' they shared all things, and no one knew any lack. We are not talking so much about a pooling of resources, but about the liberality from which they lived together. Together they knew and believed that God was an abundant Father, a Father they could not out give. They trusted in the Father's love for them and for others. When we truly believe this and know God's nature to be so abundant toward us His children, we will give just as freely and sow into the Kingdom economy that God has made available here and now.

The believers in Acts 4 saw giving differently because they saw one another differently. They could act on their faith because they knew they were giving out of God's storehouse, not their own. They gave freely from a place of oneness with God and one another.; and because of this, not only did their families know no lack but the whole family of God around them knew no lack. This is what we can expect all around the world when we too operate together in a

Kingdom economy, our uncommon community of cared-for "family" will only grow that much larger. Through unity, God's economy always multiplies and never divides.

When examining the passage from Acts 4, we must see it first through Kingdom eyes. This kind of belief system is not meant to be applied on a political level. It is when we blend these Kingdom principles with the control of politics and legislation that we end up throwing the baby out with the bath water and fighting for the capitalism of the world to avoid what might appear like a politically negative system. The Kingdom is not a system, but a culture of faith we can live into because of a love so perfect from our Father. I will make this very clear, this is not a "share the pot" system to be enforced and legislated. This is Kingdom economics, learning to see economics in a new light through faith in who our Father really is. This is not a foundation of beliefs that can or should be legislated, as faith must come out of freedom of choice, not force.

*The kind of living that the apostles modeled is not a limit, but an opportunity to choose a Kingdom that still capitalizes, but does so at an even greater rate through community, rather than capitalist individuals. The Kingdom breeds a supernatural kind of multiplication that overcomes the division of building one's own. The apostles knew how to live in and out of an uncommon unity, in Spirit and in truth, even in their economics. We cannot keep our economics separate from our Kingdom, and Jesus prayed that His people, of His kingdom, would become one in an uncommon unity. Economics are not the exception unless our hearts are divided to let economics rule. Jesus said it, even commanded it Himself, **'Freely you have received, freely give' (Matt. 10:8)."***

Generosity

"...in a great trial of affliction the abundance of their joy and their deep poverty abounded in the riches of their liberality. For I bear witness that according to their ability, yes, and beyond their ability, they were freely willing." (2 Corinthians 8:2-3)

Or, The Message translation says it clearly and poignantly:

"Fierce troubles came down on the people of those churches, pushing them to the very limit. The trial exposed their true colors: They were incredibly happy, though desperately poor. The pressure triggered something totally unexpected: an outpouring of pure and generous gifts. I saw it for myself. They gave offerings of whatever they could— far more than they could afford!" (2 Corinthians 8:2-3 The Message)

If we will keep our freedoms while also reforming society in a way that empowers people into a family structure, generosity is key. We cannot build a family structure or reform the socioeconomics of poverty or culture as a whole without choosing generosity to be at the forefront.

One of the number one issues discussed in politics and government is that of taxes. There are various models of government that each legislate economics and socioeconomics differently through more or fewer taxes (more on that later). We would not need such arguments if we as believers were walking like the early church did. We would already be giving the world a more free government of hope if we were leading with our generosity more consistently, more freely.

I believe our capitalism and free market to be essential in furthering liberty and empowerment, however I also believe we have to reform such with how we choose to use our freedoms. There is corruption and injustice all through societies and nations around the world. But, we are the ones who hold the key. Let's not make the government do our job for us, let's be a government of hope. We are the ones, in our generosity, that hold the key to justice for others.

Magnifying Boaz

Before we left Ethiopia the Lord gave me one other defining, life-message type of word that fits into building a *Family Structure* and beginning to do so through the "empty vessels."

My family and I had just come home from what we called "street church." It had been a long—but good—day and I was exhausted. I began to set my Bible down next to our bed when I heard that still, small voice of the Holy Spirit say, *"Pick it back up, I have something for you."* So I picked up my Bible and replied, "Ok, what is it?" "Ruth 2," He whispered back. "Ruth 2?" I blurted back out. "What do you want me to do with Ruth 2?" Then the Spirit closed our conversation with, *"Magnify it."*

I went to study the familiar story of Ruth 2 not knowing what new piece I would get from it. I didn't just read it, I prayed through it—over and over again. That's when I began to see the story through a slightly new angle that spoke loudly.

Ruth came into Boaz' field during a time in the world when the law stated that anyone who was poor, widowed, orphaned or a foreigner could go into a field and glean from its corners, its scraps, the extras. So, since Ruth matched several of those stigmas, she was on her way to her relative's property to glean what she could for her and Naomi. When Boaz saw Ruth, he could have just seen her as everyone else did; as a foreigner (and a Moabitess at that), as poor or as a widow. He could have just seen her need and helped fill that need as she hoped. But that's where Boaz did something different, something that launched his "Kinsman" or "family" redeemer calling.

When Boaz saw Ruth for who she really was, as faithful—as *family*—it changed the way he gave to her. Instead of just giving what was required, or what would be "enough," Boaz saw her as family and gave to her more abundantly than she needed, more abundantly than she asked, and more abundantly than what was common for the time.

Ruth was so overwhelmed by Boaz' generosity and favor that she remained at that field, became part of that house, married Boaz and together they had the son we mentioned earlier, Obed. And as you may recall, Obed became the father of Jesse. And Jesse had a son named David. And thus, the "Family Structure" was redeemed and given new life, all because of the abundant spirit of generosity of Boaz, who loved and cared for Ruth not according to what was enough for her need, but he gave to her liberally like a member of the family. That generosity made her a more integral part of the family, and helped birth the rest of the kingdom heritage that changed the world. Simply put, Boaz' generosity further built a family structure.

I believe in this time and to bring about a living government of hope we need to magnify the generous way that Boaz gave to Ruth. When we do so freely and consistently, more people—no matter their circumstance or social class—will feel like family, *like they belong.*

Our economics and free market capitalism is important, but it must become our servant and not our master. Capitalism doesn't mean we need to capitalize on the marginalized, like the potential Ruths all around us today. Rather, it's an opportunity to freely love them with a generosity of spirit that makes them feel empowered and like they belong. Some call it "Compassion Capitalism" (*book by Harold Eberle, Compassion Capitalism*); I've often referred to it as something of a "Golden Rule Capitalism." No matter how we phrase it, we don't have to go to the other extremes of legislated socialism to bring the justice that people deserve and that the world needs. In fact, the world needs our free market capitalism; it's just that it also needs us to lead such with a Boaz type spirit of abundant generosity.

Many are tired of the corruption that highlights culture's greed and many are trying to fight back through other forms of legislation. However, the only way to get rid of the enemy's corruption in the world is to overcome its lynch pins of selfishness and fear. We overcome those lynch pins and much of what divides us when we choose to lead through generosity.

Uncommon Unity

"If you want to go fast, go alone. If you want to go far, go together." - African Proverb

After years of living a missions lifestyle and daily living by faith, I can truly say that one of God's greatest, most consistent and underrated forms of provision is through community—the people around you who love and believe in you. There have been too many times to count that we have passed through very narrow days, and seasons as a whole. And God has had a community around us that became what the ravens were to Elijah, bringing him meat in the wilderness so he could continue his road forward. A lot of people are one hard circumstance away from the bottom, unless they have family-like community around them as their net. Community is a protection and support, and as it was in the book of Acts, it is a most powerful form of multiplication. Ruth experienced both of those dynamics on the way to the family structure that flowed through the lives of her and Boaz.

Multiplication always takes two. We have to have more than ourselves to move the needle in a consistent way, no matter how much we are doing with our part. That's why the oneness that the community in Acts 4 experienced was so powerful. Their unity wasn't based on similarity or proximity, it was not a horizontal unity by worldly standards; no, it was a unity of heart and soul, where they were in sync and in tune with one another because they each were in sync and in tune with the Holy Spirit.

When we each breathe in oneness with the Spirit, we breathe in oneness with others whose breath is aligned in the same way. The Spirit of God is Who united this uncommon community, and truly, following the Holy Spirit is the truest form of progress. We'll touch more on that later in the chapter. What is vital is that not only were these apostles generous individually, but their generosity of spirit was community-wide.

In Jesus' final prayer in John 17:20-24, He prayed that believers would be "one" so that the world may believe. I contend that is exactly what was happening through this Acts 4 community. They were living the answer to His prayer. They were all operating out of such oneness with the Spirit, and therefore with one another. This gave them freedom from the self and freedom from the fear of not having enough because it wasn't any of them alone who were giving. Because within such a community they were both giving and receiving at the same time, a never ending overflow of multiplication compared to the division that selfishness and fear have driven us towards today.

Plenty of people give unselfishly in different ways all the time, but if we as believers decided to do so in sync and in tune with one another across a city, a culture, or a nation—that is when and where a government of hope is birthed for the world to experience God's family structure—through generosity, together.

What happens is we become a cross section of interwoven threads. We all have something to give, and often we all have abundance of *something*. How often we look back at the story of Joseph and the strategy he had to redeem Egypt and surrounding areas during the famine. We try and re-create these with "Joseph-type storehouse" models all over. Though this is a really good thing, I actually believe the cross section of a generous community we're called to cultivate can and will become a modern version of Joseph's storehouse during difficult times in the world. When a physical structure type of storehouse is built around a large stock of food, there is a limit to that. But when that storehouse is made out of a crossover-community of generous givers across a city or region, there is perpetual multiplication that will not run out.

This is how we mend the nets to help redeem the world, we become a family structure based storehouse that is not reliant on one person, ministry or church, but is a broader community across a city, operating in uncommon oneness and generosity. That is how Acts 4 brought us the testimony of oneness, great grace, and no one having any lack.

The other important part about a community learning to give freely together in this way is the need for holistic giving. This means that our giving is not relegated only to dollars and cents, but how pertinent it is that our treasures are given in combination with our time and our talents. For instance, instead of a business only writing a check to a group to help support those in poverty, what if that same business had an "empowerment track" that opened the door for internships and mentoring. This way, a few of those receiving the needed funds would get access to vision and a purpose that may give them hope and motivation—and what is more, they would also gain community, a group of people outside their current circumstances that help guide them out of the margins simply by walking forward together.

It's through these simple types of things all working together that we can build a family structure. And that is what this group of apostles did. It was no common form of unity they walked in, they redefined it and proved it through their overwhelming generosity. And what a testimony sprang from it—*no one had any lack*. Imagine saying this about your city, culture or nation ten years from now.

Authentic vs. Counterfeit

The true enemy we're facing isn't on the right or the left of the political spectrum. See, the enemy doesn't take sides, he hides and deceives and tries to play both sides against one another. So anytime there is something like the incredible testimony in the book of Acts, or threat of it coming to life again—the enemy will not bring a dark, obvious opposite to oppose it, rather, he'll work to bring layers of counterfeit so as to woo us off track like a wolf in sheep's clothing, with mirrored components of the authentic. However, they lack the redemptive value because they come from a different source.

Whenever we have the near possibility of such a beautifully authentic reality, there are always the counterfeit versions that come masquerading as one of them. That is where we find many of the "Isms" of today's world. And yet, even with such threats to our necessary freedom, we can be encouraged that if there is such a timely draw to these counterfeits *and* they are emerging closer than ever before, then the authentic reality those "isms" are counterfeited from must also be available right at our doorstep. But it's up to us to use our freedom and answer that call to bring that authentic reality to life, *before* the counterfeits come barging through. We must use and give our freedom more fully while we are so blessed to have it. The more we use our freedom this way the more of it we will keep, and the more it will multiply. But if we're passive, we give the counterfeits an open door that we could have closed.

Socialism

Socialism is the counterfeit of what happened in Acts 4. There is one major difference that makes it so; in the book of Acts the community gives and shares generously out of freedom of choice, which as we've talked about cultivates a multiplication of all that is being shared. But with socialism, the difference is that it is forced upon the whole of society through legislation, robbing us of freedom and hope.

Freedom vs. legislation, the choice is really ours, and we make that choice long before we vote. There is selfishness in both extremes of capitalism and socialism. On one extreme it's about me, what I can gain and keep. On the other extreme of socialism it's about the government doing the giving for me and taking unwarranted control. Both are selfish, and that's why there continues to be such a war in our culture, because the real enemy plays on our selfishness and tries to divide us so that our house cannot stand.

But, if we will simply live the model Jesus showed us and give freely, generously *before* it is taxed and taken from us, we'll start to be the authentic answer in between; maintaining our freedom and free market while also empowering the rest of society in a just and loving way. And through such we'll build a *Family Structure* that is the opposite of the division the enemy is trying to bring. Freedom is the difference. We can change the social sphere of society without surrendering our freedom to the hope-robbing counterfeit of socialism. We just have to use our freedom for everyone, and not just for me.

Progressivism

Most of us want to be progressive in some way, shape or form. We don't want to remain in the mud of the past while God brings a fresh wave. However, not all forward movement is from God.

If we are not in oneness with the Holy Spirit and actively allowing Him a living place in our life to direct our steps, to be our breath, to hear His voice; then we will look to progress by more carnal thinking instead. We will substitute good for the best, or man's ways for God's ways. Much of progressivism among the church is simply believers conforming more to society's bend than the leading of the Holy Spirit. We are all constantly progressing in some form; it's up to us whether that progress is led by the Spirit or by the influences of the world's forms of justice.

God loves justice even more than those leading the social justice movements all around us, so we can trust that His Spirit will always lead us into the authentic kinds. Society should not be dictating our progress in this area, *the Holy Spirit should*. And with Him, believers—like those in Acts 4—will be leading the way.

Globalism

As we traveled and lived overseas I was far too aware of the reality of the "ugly American" concept. It was the last thing I ever wanted to perpetuate. I wanted to serve other nations, other cultures, other people—not pronounce that America was or is the best at the expense of other beloved people.

I still believe those things, but not at the expense of America either. Globalism has come as a counterfeit to us having a more selfless world perspective. We do need to get outside of our self; we do need to see other cultures and nations as different, not necessarily better or worse. But that does not mean we weaken America to do so. In fact, part of the foundation of America in this way was to love our neighbors and the nations. We use our freedom to wash their feet. We use our strength to serve. We strengthen our house for the sake of also taking care of other nations around the world. You are no help to your neighbors in need if you do not take care of your own house too, for you wouldn't have a stable, secure place to love them in, or from. When we adopted our daughters from Ethiopia we first had to show a strong family and home *so that* we could be who they deserved. The same is true for the nations.

Humanism

Jesus gave Himself, became poor and as nothing for the sake of humanity. He gave Himself as God's Son to overcome the sin that separates us from God so that we too could be God's sons and daughters. Humanism is a sneaky counterfeit. As it has made its subtle way in, it has tried to rob the power of God's love. It lifts humanity above God, above truth—but it won't tell you that of course.

I believe one of the greatest deceptions (counterfeits) of our day will be the lure of humanism that does one simple thing; it places the second commandment higher than the first.

Our first and greatest commandment is to love God with all our heart, mind, soul and strength. Our second commandment is to love our neighbors as ourselves. The order matters—*a lot*! See, when we love God first and foremost and keep the right order, then we go out to love mankind our love will transform people into God's image. But when we flip the order and love people first, we remove our plumb line of truth, and instead of seeing people transformed by the love of God, soon we start to conform God into man's image. Instead of making our love a path for healing and transformation, our love simply becomes a method of inclusion and we've rendered God's love and Jesus' sacrifice as nothing.

It is only a very subtle difference at first. But it leads to one of the gravest deceptions. The order of these commandments matter a great deal, yet the culture around us is trying to slowly flip them right underneath our nose. Our love for our neighbor will make no eternal difference if it is not tethered to the truth of loving God more than man.

Universalism

There is only one way to the Father, through Jesus Christ. He is the Way, the Truth, and the Life. (John 14:4) Jesus is the Prince of Peace whose government, and rule, knows no end. (Isaiah 9:7) So, the counterfeit the enemy has planted in the world is to create a false, worldly kind of peace through harmony of religions and false gods. The enemy tries to blur the lines so that the government of The Prince of Peace won't overtake his territory, acting as if it is all the same anyway. That couldn't be further from the truth, and believing such keeps many people from finding *The Way* as the person of Jesus. Universalism is the counterfeit that you are already included no matter what you believe, while Jesus brings us a truth that says you already belong, only believe.

In truth, most if not all of these "ism's" are counterfeit forms of the kind of true, uncommon unity that Jesus prayed for in John 17 before going to the cross. The world, the enemy, is trying to counterfeit the answer to Jesus' most powerful prayer because he knows what will happen if we come together in the Spirit of God to become *the real thing;* the answer Jesus Himself prayed for and the answer that the Acts 4 church modeled.

If we will resist the temptations of the counterfeits and step into the real truth that Jesus prayed for, it will cause the world to believe!

> **"I do not pray for these alone, but also for those who will believe in Me through their word; that they all may be one, as You, Father, are in Me, and I in You; that they also may be one in Us, that the world may believe that You sent Me."** **(John 17:20-21)**

If we are going to lead the way in our culture with a government of hope that actually transforms people and societies, it is right at our doorstep and the testimony of the Acts 4 church is ready to be welcomed in again, *for such a time as this.* The oneness and generosity they modeled give us a living blueprint of what the Family Structure can look like among us today. But there are two key ingredients that are absolutely necessary: Uncommon unity and a spirit of generosity.

> **"Now the multitude of those who believed were of one heart and one soul; neither did anyone say that any of the things he possessed was his own, but they had all things in common. And with great power the apostles gave witness to the resurrection of the Lord Jesus. And great grace was upon them all. Nor was there anyone among them who lacked..."** **(Acts 4:32-34)**

Chapter 7:

A Hopeful Generation

> "Then the word of the Lord came to me, saying: 'Before I formed you in the womb I knew you; Before you were born I sanctified you; I ordained you a prophet to the nations.' Then said I: 'Ah, Lord God! Behold I cannot speak, for I am a youth.' But the Lord said to me: 'Do not say, 'I am a youth, For you shall go to all to whom I send you, and whatever I command you, you shall speak. Do not be afraid of their faces, for I am with you to deliver you,' says the Lord."
> (Jeremiah 1:4-8)

This "blessing" that God gave Jeremiah is not too different in nature from a similar blessing and belief that I received when I was young—which marked and changed my life forever.

The youth of our communities and nations are part of that most vital entry point to usher in a true and lasting government of hope. The term and definition for "youth" can be very different from nation to nation, so I'm not just speaking of one set or defined age group. I am speaking *for* the younger generation as a whole, and perhaps *to* the younger generation as a whole. The essence of why and how can both be summed up in a simple, if not familiar, internal craving that we all have and need: *To be believed in.*

I was one of the fortunate ones growing up, in that not only did I have a lot of unconditional love around me, but I was thoroughly blessed to have a lot of family and older close friends in my life who believed in me. They let me know it and they showed it. And I will never be the same because of it. In fact, I've spent the better part of the last twenty plus years trying to impart that same "believed in" message to everyone I could, young and old, because I realize that far too few people have had the "believed in" experience that I was privileged to have.

I probably didn't even know at what level their belief impacted me in the moment. Feeling "believed in," often without cognitively knowing you do or don't, is a basic human need for our inner person. We rarely say that, but when we feel believed in it sets us free to live beyond the glass ceiling of our lives, our circumstances, and even our culture. And when we do not feel such belief behind us we can tend to gradually build up walls of self-doubt and insecurity that become a filter affecting almost every part of our lives.

To believe in someone in a way that they can *feel* is one of the most powerful gifts we can offer, and that it is one of the most necessary basic needs that the younger generation across the world is silently crying out for. They may not show it and you may not show it, as we can be very good at becoming self-sufficient and rebuilding those internal places of lack with other forms of self-worth. But the truth is that we all crave to have those in our corner who genuinely believe in us, those who both say it and show it.

Having those people in my life changed me. It set me free to dream and believe that anything was possible. I was sending in shoe ideas to Reebok at age seven, starting my own business at eleven, trying to convince a major newspaper in Denver to hire a youth sports columnist when I was thirteen, and speaking at and organizing youth events and conferences by seventeen. And that continued over the years. I never stopped to think about how ridiculous some of those swings might look because of the support and belief of those around me. Even when I swung and missed, it wasn't devastating. It became a stepping-stone of a learning experience to help me leap to the next.

The belief of others in my life helped me know that God believed in me, like He did Jeremiah in the passage above; even while Jeremiah was still so young. God did the same with the prophet Samuel at a very young age, and many others all throughout the Bible. But my favorite story of giving such belief away to empower someone comes from the origins of God's family, and it strategically and powerfully wove its way into my life and story as well—and eventually through my life and family to others.

The Father's Blessing

I've written about this historical and Biblical form of imparting belief many times because it is a part of me, and, because I believe in the power of what happens when it is a part of others as well. I believe it is absolutely vital that the younger generation be shown this kind of belief by those around them, whether that be Dad, Mom, a relative, or a friend (younger or older); as I believe this generation plays a key part in the government of hope that we will all raise up together. Below is the story I share of such from my book, *The Life Giver, in the chapter, "Creative Authority," (pgs. 141-144)*:

> "This is the father's blessing that began with Abraham and was passed down through Isaac and Jacob. The father's blessing began in my life when my dad asked if they could throw me a "blessing party" for my 16th

birthday and encouraged me to read Genesis 27:1-40 to prepare.

'Then his father Isaac said to him (Jacob), 'Come near now and kiss me, my son.' And he came near and kissed him; and he smelled the smell of his clothing, and blessed him and said: 'Surely, the smell of my son is like the smell of a field which the Lord has blessed. Therefore may God give you of the dew of heaven, of the fatness of the earth, and plenty of grain and wine. Let peoples serve you, and nations bow down to you. Be master over your brethren, and let your mother's sons bow down to you. Cursed be everyone who curses you, and blessed be those who bless you" (Genesis 27:26-29).**

Isaac did not offer a blessing to Jacob from a known script. He blessed him with what God had put in his heart. Isaac blessed Jacob toward purpose, with faith, and prophesied great life to come. Now that is using creative authority. Isaac spoke life into Jacob and his future through the father's blessing. Jacob went on to live an abundantly fruitful life of purpose and impact. Isaac's blessing was more than words; it was God's power come to life because it was given with faith. Not long after this blessing and prophecy of life to come, Jacob himself had an intimate and special encounter with God at Bethel, a time often refer to as Jacob's ladder (see Gen. 28).

When my dad approached me with this story and proposed the 'blessing party' for my birthday, I must admit that I was less than enthused. I tried not to show it on the outside, but I did not initially have a lot of faith in this kind of party's potential. I was remembering back to a 13th birthday bash that I thoroughly enjoyed. We rented a rec center to accommodate more than 70 friends from youth group and school. And among other fun memories of that party, we took over the city on a widespread scavenger hunt. So, for my 16th, my fleshly perspective had me dreaming of something grand again. My mom and dad were thinking of something grand as well, but from a perspective I could not see yet. However, I could see in my dad's eyes how important this blessing party was to him, so, reluctantly, I agreed.

I read the story of Isaac, Jacob, and Esau and still did not think much of it. The night of my birthday blessing came around, and my parents had invited a number of family friends. They included a bit of an extended family from church or other families my mom and dad had been involved in ministry with for years. Everyone went around the room and took turns sharing with me. They shared memories, stories, areas of gifting, purpose, and value that they observed in my life. They spoke words of encouragement and love. It was really special. But what happened next, I will never be able to fully communicate. My parents took creative authority through their connection with God to give me new life and to speak life into the future that was ahead of me.

They had been praying for weeks, if not months, over this blessing for me. My dad wrote out a prayer of blessing that was almost three pages long. In the blessing he offered me love, belief, value, purpose, and foresight into God's potential future for my life. He blessed me to be who God had made me to be, rather than who he, my mom, or the world wanted me to be. He set me free to live the life God had purposed me for and gave me his blessing to go forward. This was huge for me, more than I even knew at the time. Like Jacob, the power of life that was injected into me at the time of the blessing has continued to be revealed more and more with each passing year. But even at that time, something changed dramatically...

...This father's blessing was perhaps the most significant turn of events in my life, after my receiving Christ and the baptism of the Holy Spirit. That next year after the blessing was jam-packed with God and the overflowing of new life. However, it was also the year my dad passed away, three weeks shy of my 17th birthday, while he was on a missions trip in Vietnam. Three days before he left, I had the opportunity to return the blessing, not just as a son to a father, but while we wept hand in hand as brothers in Christ. He died unexpectedly on what was one of many frequent trips to Vietnam. But before my dad left this earth, he exercised his God-given creative authority to join the Life Giver and give me new and more abundant life. I have never been the same since that blessing, and still today, I watch new life come forward from what was given the day of the blessing. I do not know how I would have made it through my dad's sudden death if not for the life that had just been given to me."

One of the ways we will see a lasting government of hope come forward in this new era we are in is by believing in the younger generation in a way that breathes life into their identity. My dad offered one specific quote in his blessing over me that I will never forget. He said:

"I hope you never believe that just because you're not like me in every area of life that I think you're a lesser person. That's a common belief among sons of type-A dads. In fact, I believe the very best hope for the LeTourneau name lies in the very ways that you are different from me."

This statement is revolutionary. How infrequently do we unconditionally bless and believe in another person so outwardly, despite the differences in their life. And these aren't just any differences, but recognizing God breathed special identity hidden in me that was different than him and blessing me to be who God made me to be rather than try and live up to him or his ways.

That is the opposite of what happens in many "fathering" types of relationships. Actually, it's the opposite of what happens in many of our relationships period. We often want people to conform to our image, rather than help them fulfill the image of God that He made them in. It's the root of God's image in someone—especially this emerging, younger generation—that must be empowered to come forth and live hope out loud. We have to be this for one another. We can't mire in our insecurities any longer and let some of the beautiful, God-created differences within us lie dormant without having permission to shine to the world!

"Behold, I will send you Elijah the prophet before the coming of the great and dreadful day of the Lord. And he will turn the hearts of the fathers to the children, an the hearts of the children to their fathers..." (Malachi 4:5-6)

Four Core Values of Empowerment

Over the years, I've tried to dissect the blessing into what exactly God imparted to me through my parents. Though intangible, it produced much tangible change and fruit. We've actually developed empowerment curriculum and activation resources called *The Culture Purple: empower.ED*. It's written in language that isn't only faith based, so that way we can take it into any nation, any sphere, to anyone in the world to impart identity and empower them to discover and live out their unique purpose in the world. In this, I've found there to be Four Core Values that we must rise up and offer the emerging generation in order to be a government of hope, together.

You are Valued

This is to recognize and affirm that someone has value simply for who they are. It is to see and bless the fact that they carry intrinsic worth just by walking into a room. It is to communicate to them their value to us and others. It is to remind them the value that their life already does and will bring to the world. It is to make sure they know that they are valued by God, and that He put value in them that far supersedes anything they could ever do to earn it. They are valued for who they are.

You are Loved

Unconditional love has become one of the rarer things in this world, yet it remains one of our heart's greatest needs. This kind of unmeasured love is the bloodline of what we are offering someone in the blessing. We may or may not always approve of what they do, but that does not and will not change our love for who they are. We can communicate this to people freely because this is God's perspective of love towards us and we have an entire generation around us that needs to feel this love from us to help them know how God feels about them. They don't have to earn this love from God, or us, they just have to receive it. Again, this doesn't mean we approve of all actions, beliefs or decisions, but it does mean that we are imparting a love that covers those things and even transforms those things. We must make sure the emerging generation knows they are loved simply for who they are in our lives.

You have Purpose

How much more hope do you have when you feel a sense of purpose? This sense of purpose is a game-changer, because it helps us value ourselves. Purpose can be small or large. It can be unique, joint, temporary, part of a calling and so much more. Purpose is an innate desire in every life, so we must take the time to invest in a person's purpose. We have to point to it when they don't see it, remind them of it when they forget, support them when they step towards it, and help keep hope alive even when they fail.

A purposeful generation is a more self-accountable and self-motivated generation. It's hard to do on our own because there are so many things to overcome on each of our own purpose journeys. We need people to come behind us and beside us and bless the unique purpose we carry. Imagine a city or nation changed because you lived your purpose and dream. Imagine if they lived theirs. Imagine a whole generation of youth not just coming of age, but brimming with God's unique purpose in each of them.

I Believe in You

We're back to where we started in this chapter, the power and importance of believing in someone. How often do you remind people of your belief in them? How often do you think they crave it, knowingly or unknowingly? How can you start showing them, let alone telling them? We need the generation coming after us and around us to absolutely *know* that we believe in them. This helps to rid us of our fears, insecurities, pride, or control. You name it, this kind of loving belief goes right to the root. We don't have to fight to prove ourselves the wrong way when we know there is someone who believes in us for the right ones. Let them hear it, don't keep it to yourself. To give someone belief is to give them hope. To give them hope is to give them reason to step forward, and to keep stepping forward in meaningful ways. They were created for a special purpose, let's believe in them in that way!

A Key Ingredient

The Father's Blessing was a key ingredient to all we saw happen in Ethiopia, and elsewhere since. It helped spark what became the *Family Structure* across the streets of Ethiopia. It's the oil we took and poured out to the empty vessels. It's something we've tried to give generously to people near and far. When people feel valued for who they are, it's amazing how seamlessly they step into their identity and the unique way that naturally fits into the uncommon unity God forms us to be as the Body of Christ.

We gave the Father's Blessing to those first eight orphans we spent time with, starting with the oldest boy. As we spoke it over his life in front a number of other people it was like watching the sun rise on his life. Immediately this thirteen-year-old boy stepped up and helped us impart the same into each of the other kids. Then, these kids helped us impart such a "Father's Blessing" to the kids on the streets. We would rent out restaurants sometimes for some of these moments. I'll never forget a handful of kids began to come up, and after receiving it, took this simple piece of folded up paper, held it up proudly and asked us to take a photo, as if they were posing with their diploma. Much later on many of these street kids did indeed get their diploma. Some even graduated with the best grades in their district, and some have gone on to start businesses, go to college, return to their families and to bring hope to all these places—a hope that they themselves didn't even have before.

However, these "Father's Blessings" became a prophetic declaration over their lives that they took to heart and lived out once they realized that they, too, were valued, loved, had purpose, and especially, that we believed in them.

Finishing the Story: Esau

"When Esau heard the words of his father, he cried with an exceedingly great and bitter cry, and said to his father, 'Bless me—me also, O my father!'" (Genesis 27:34)

When Jacob received his "Father's Blessing" from Isaac, it was because Esau had lost hope, lost vision, lost purpose and gave away his birthright. Yet for me, Esau has always been my primary focal point of the story. Why? Because as the above verse tells us, when Esau actually saw Jacob receive the blessing, he let out a loud and bitter cry, **"Bless me—me also, O my father!"**

If we could listen with the ears of our hearts, we would hear this cry from those all around us, young and old. It is a cry that we have all had at some point in our lives. It's the cry of a birthright, to know that we have worth and a purpose.

I always imagine that scene. I see Esau staring at Isaac, crying out, and Isaac sorrowfully shaking his head, saddened that he couldn't meet his son's need. But I also picture our

Everlasting Father above Esau, saying, *"I love you. I value you. I believe in you!"* But Esau can't look up, he can't receive the Father who is pursuing him because Esau is so focused on Isaac, on man, on the world; searching for value and significance. Many of us, and those around us, won't allow ourselves to receive the Father Who has been pursuing us the whole time because we are focused and striving for man or the world to fill that void.

Again, Esau was locked in on Isaac, his earthly father, when he cried out this desperate longing for identity. Under the culture of the time, Isaac did not have another blessing to give. But now, through Jesus, *we do*!

For all those around us who share that same cry of Esau we can step into the role of Isaac, a father or mother in nature, and speak that blessing, that value, love, purpose and belief over a life and set them free *so that* they can take their eyes off of needing such from man, or the world, and receive the Everlasting Father Who has been pursuing them, loving them, and believing in them this whole time.

We can set people free to live their worth and purpose. The cry of Esau is all around us—especially in the younger generation. If we will step into this role of "Isaac" for others, we can give identity back to a generation who will be a government of hope in their city, culture, and nation; just as we saw happen in Ethiopia.

God has always found so much power and purpose in this Father's Blessing that He used it to empower His family from the beginning. Before Jesus began His ministry we read of God virtually stopping time and opening the heavens just to say over His Son, **"This is My beloved Son, in whom I am well pleased. (Matthew 3:17)**

If the Father thought even Jesus needed to hear it, feel it, and receive it; How many around you, around the world, are waiting to hear the same?

Chapter 8:

A Culture of Life

I sat on the stage of our congressional forum/debate in the middle of two democratic and much more liberal candidates. I myself was running as an independent with no party preference, but many of my views were and are shaped by more conservative values. There were many subjects that night that tested my backbone, speaking in a room that was almost one hundred percent "blue."

I personally didn't mind this so much as I love to get beyond the labels of democrat and republican, red or blue; but the reality in that room was quite evident that most were indeed aligned with a partisan "side" and that was never clearer than when the topic of abortion had its turn.

I tried to speak into the subject beyond a pre-decided black or white stance, because as much as I value life from conception I also believe that like with most other issues, we must go deeper to the roots to see them healed. Most in the room couldn't hear that, some who had been warm turned much colder towards me, as I was now possibly an affront to their beliefs—though I think the conversation goes a little further than we usually take it. While most in the room that night couldn't hear the nuance of life I was advocating for, I received an e-mail later on during our campaign from someone who had seen and listened to what I tried to share. She greatly appreciated my perspective on several issues, and though she said she could never vote for a man who might possibly stand against abortion in some way, she actually listened to and repeated back to me my stance on the subject; listening beyond the assigned "side" of my answer and hearing the holistic approach at which I believe we must look deeper. I might not have had her vote, but I sure appreciated that she actually listened—a far too rare quality in politically charged environments.

I think if we all listened more we could actually create more solutions. We still may not agree on a subject as big as legislating abortion, but perhaps we could learn to see a bigger picture that—if lived out in culture—wouldn't altogether remove choice but could help create enough life in our culture to slow down, then prevent, and eventually help stop abortion all together.

Let me continue by saying that as a Dad of seven I am 100% Pro-life, or at least I seek to be. But my perspective of what that means continues to grow. While I strongly believe the atrocities of abortion to be on par with the Holocaust as one of the gravest injustices and mistakes of the last century, I also believe that the way we are fighting against it has too often (not always) become carnal and political. We have allowed, and even perpetuated abortion to become right vs. left, red vs. blue. This has allowed the opposition to largely throw out the truth of life as nothing more than the opinion of "the other side." But this argument is beyond pro-life vs. pro-choice, and we must be too.

This is about our need for a holistic culture of life that goes beyond a law or piece of legislation; a culture that realizes life is in what we say, who we take care of, how we take care of them and the pro-active steps we take that help more people choose LIFE! And yes, this very much includes the unborn, but the root of abortion goes much deeper into the value system of our culture and individual lives of how we value every person near and far. The more we cultivate life *before* the choice, the more people who will learn to choose it. We all birth this culture every single day with what can seem to be the most insignificant of choices, words and actions. And it is in those small words, choices and actions that we will all, together, birth a true movement of LIFE.

We can only re-frame this discussion if we as followers of Jesus become less politically dependent, becoming more consistent in a holistic pro-life approach across culture— abortion and beyond. Life, specifically "Pro-life," is a value system that spans from conception to eternity.

What does this look like? It wills us to venture further, deeper into more poverty care, into *how* we embrace immigrants and refugees, our perspective of capital punishment, how we more widely and consistently open up our families to the adoption and foster care system, and how we educate people with the value of life *pro-actively* before their choice, helping lead their choice instead of merely condemning them for condemning a life. Darkness cannot cast out darkness and neither can condemnation cast out condemnation.

We need a refreshed, holistic, life-giving approach to fighting abortion at the root level. Otherwise, we'll always be reliant on who has the Oval office, who has the Judges, and who has the House. Government leaders can help lay important framework, but we must let go of the tug-o-war rope long enough to get our hands dirty, heal the roots and plant new seeds in this really vital soil.

Known

"Before I formed you in the womb I knew you; before you were born I sanctified you..." (Jeremiah 1:5)

I want to revisit this verse we started the last chapter with as well. Look at what God is saying to Jeremiah: **"*BEFORE* I formed you in the womb, I *KNEW* you"** (emphasis mine). **"*BEFORE* you were born, I sanctified you"** (emphasis mine).

God recognized, valued and sanctified Jeremiah's life *BEFORE* he was even formed in the womb. To any believer, this should be as clear an indication as any about when and where life truly begins. Can you imagine God already *knowing* you, liking you, loving you at that time? Can you comprehend the reality of being known by God at such a time? Can you imagine the Father's heart when this precious, known life to him is so quickly, sometimes frivolously snatched from who he knows it to be? Our eyes, perspective and knowledge of life only goes so far. We are too often making our "choice" off of very limited information. If we are honest with ourselves, we don't really *know* the life we're choosing for or against, *but God does*!

As a dad of seven children, my wife and I have six daughters and one son. Two of our daughters are adopted, and I have had the immense privilege of being right there and actively involved in labor and delivery for each of our five biological kids—some of the most special and miraculous moments of my life.

Each labor and delivery was very different—which my wife knows far better than I do! We (all credit to my wife of course) have had one smooth, quick hospital birth, one birth in a small Ethiopian hospital, one nerve-wracking emergency C-section, one challenging home birth (God bless my wife!) and one incredible, almost supernatural home birth. Each one goes to show that there are different ways to give life, various challenges and processes to birth life, and different moments of fighting for life even when it's not easy, and sometimes downright scary. But giving life, protecting life and fighting for life—in all their forms—are all worth it!

I can honestly say that apart from God and His word, that women are the ones who have shaped my opinions on such matters. I've grown up primarily with my mom, as my dad passed away when I was sixteen. I have one sister who I am very close to. My wife, Destiny, has experienced and made the self-sacrificing choice for life through some of the most real "choice" moments women face. I have six daughters who I cherish, who I always want to have the freedom of choice, but who have shaped their choices around the value of life. I recently had the overwhelming joy of actually catching and receiving our daughter into this world, a miracle of life that marks you forever.

During our time in Ethiopia, right in the middle of our adoption of our two older girls, and only nine months after our second daughter was born; we were presented with a surprising choice of our own. It was not the choice of abortion, but it was the choice of giving life in the face of death. It was not easy, not because the life we chose wasn't worth it, but because the choice and the process of life required sacrifice. We had to put life before self. Actually, we didn't have to; we were free to, and chose to.

Our social worker for our adoption was visiting our home in Ethiopia. That year, with our daughter born and our two adopted daughters joyously coming into the family, we were going from a family of three to a family of six. Before our social worker wrapped up our home study that day, our moment of choice happened. She said that she had just been made aware of one orphaned infant in their transition home.

The baby was transitioning towards a family who was adopting him, but she, the social worker, had just been made aware of the baby's incredible special needs. The needs were so severe that the nurses at the transition home could no longer take care of him. And with his special needs, the agency didn't feel like the adoption could go on as planned, so this little special needs infant needed an emergency home and care-taking.

His name at that time was Sidamo. He had been born about six weeks premature and abandoned in a field. They didn't know what his special needs were except that he shook and trembled most of the time, shrieked piercing cries and screams, and couldn't make eye contact; his eyes glazed over like he was blind.

Our social worker asked if we would be willing to take him for a time until a long-term family or situation could be arranged. We were already in the middle of a lot of family transition, but God made it clear it was the right thing to do. We didn't have any medical equipment or special training, we were totally unprepared in almost all tangible ways—*but God*! We had God, prayer, faith, grace, love, truth, and many similar but powerful intangibles God had taught us to live on. We took baby Sidamo in and applied all the spiritual and natural care we could. I go into much further detail in my book, *The Life Giver*.

It was at times one of the hardest experiences of our lives. We re-named him Samuel while he was with us so as to give him a new name and a new hope, one of promise. We fought for him, prayed over him, saw a prayer time over him bring immediate healing to his eyes as they changed dramatically and he suddenly began to make eye contact with us for the first time. We were in a battle for a life that we had to choose and re-choose every single day, sometimes many times per day and some extra-tough nights.

We had Samuel for six months, six of the hardest months of our adult lives. Then our cousins from California felt moved by God to adopt him. They had a lot of experience in their family working with those with special needs, and though we didn't know what this baby's needs were yet, they were willing to say yes to a life!

Samuel left us to go back to America with our cousins, his forever family. They officially named him Micah. They now had access to medical care and a diagnosis that was not available to us previously. Though he seemed much better, relatively speaking, than when we received him six months before; Micah was immediately diagnosed with cerebral palsy, as well as failure to thrive, severe stomach issues and much more. He was put on 24-hours per day Valium and a 24-hours per day feeding tube. If this is what he needed at six months old we were left to imagine all the miracles God did during those six months to keep him alive.

The real miracle is the life and joy he now brings to his forever family. He lights up the room, communicates wherever he goes and really, he is just a ball of life! He still has a number of medical complications that his family faithfully battles through for him, but Micah truly is a testimony to the miracle of *choosing* life, not just once, but choosing life every day.

Choosing life is rarely easy, no matter the circumstances. But with some perspective, and a lot of God's grace, you are choosing so many years of so many different kinds of life and impact that will flow through that one little choice, that person. Every life matters. We must get beyond fighting just over the legislative piece of for or against, and begin to shape culture in a way that values life at all levels, in all places. We must be there for the people in our community because choosing life isn't easy, and we can't do it alone. Many people can't make the choice to be *for* a life if we are not first, *for* them.

Reforming Our Cultural Value System

It can be easy to have an opinion that is politically against abortion, what is not easy is living a holistic value system of life. I'm learning and growing in this as well, but it's a worthwhile pursuit. If we are going to be "Pro-life" then we must become more consistent with our actions, realizing that there are so many other things that breed life into every day culture.

Our moment-by-moment actions feed the choices that others are making all around us. If we are compromising life, others will more likely compromise choices of life as well. We must choose to be "pre-abortion" minded, a pro-active stance or action for life rather than just a legislative or abortion-centric one. Abortion shouldn't be a battle between life and choice; abortion should be framed for what it is—life vs. death.

If abortion centers were really only about allowing people the "choice," it would be available but wouldn't be such a growing industry. Abortion has become business, and a sick business at that; one that preys on the choice of women rather than supporting their choice and celebrating life. We cannot, and will not re-frame this conversation until we start to model life across culture in ways big and small.

Poverty Care

If it is true that many women choose abortion because they fear they won't be able to healthily support that child, then we have a real cultural opportunity before us. We, the church, can make that choice much easier for them by how we support them before the choice, during their choice, and support the life they choose after their choice. The onus isn't on them; *it's on us*. Together, our choice for compassion and generosity towards those in poverty can help eliminate poverty from being a cause of abortion. We help support their choice long before they ever have to make it.

See & Hear

If and when abortion is still permitted, I see so much power in those who are able finding ways to provide women the chance to hear the baby's heartbeat or see an ultrasound before they make that choice. Those of us who have these resources or access to them can help women better understand the life that is alive inside them. We can help women *know* the life that God already knows. We can be pro-active in ways such as these, and others, to help educate women before their choice and give them access to as much perspective as possible.

Capital Punishment

This area may be unrelated to abortion directly, but it is part of us learning to value life across the board. Capital punishment stems from a thought process that is based on "an eye for an eye" kind of justice. But as believers, our form of living justice is grace, and grace helps give and renew life. No matter what someone has done, even if it takes them years to change, I want them to have the opportunity themselves to have the choice for their life to be redeemed through Jesus. Capital punishment severely limits the option of eternal life for someone who may not know Jesus yet.

Our Words

"Death and life are in the power of the tongue, and those who love it will eat its fruit." (Proverbs 18:21)

This may seem small and insignificant compared to abortion, but our words do create life or death. This is something small but important that we can do every day to help sow more life and less death into people and culture. We can choose how we speak to people, how we speak about people, and how we speak about ourselves. Our words bring blessing or curse, and we are the ones who wield that power. These small conscious decisions are like little seeds planted each day, and even though they don't yield immediate growth, we can trust that those seeds will be part of the culture of life we build and see over time.

Foster & Adoption

We've already shared into this area a fair amount from our own story, and though it is a big, life-altering family decision for any of us who consider it; it's also life altering for the people on the other end. Whether it's foster care, adoption or orphan care; one form or another of these systems are prevalent in almost every nation. The foster system alone is overloaded with broken lives who are waiting to be chosen, lives that are headed towards a world with a lot of bad intentions if someone doesn't come along and choose life by choosing them.

Our adoptions have been some of the most wonderful, life-giving and important decisions we've ever made. With abortion, to be pro-life we often want a mother to choose the baby over self. We often have a very similar choice before us but to choose a slightly older child vs. other factors of self. I understand it's not always that easy, nor is it for some pregnant moms; but if we really want to reform abortion, then these are the kind of pro-active decisions *for* life that we need to make more often, and more consistently.

Thank you for considering *LIFE*!

> "The thief does not come except to steal, and to kill, and to destroy. I have come that they may have life, and that they may have it more abundantly." (John 10:10)

Chapter 9:

The Increase

"Of the increase of His government and peace there will be no end..." (Isaiah 9:7)

Of the increase of His government and peace there will be no end. We are entering further into this great time of increase, and it will be reflected through all our lives in practical ways that birth a superior government. This is a government that cannot be shaken. No matter what is going on in the world, this government increases through its people. When we put our dependence on something, *Someone* higher, we can then learn to be the government of hope that the world needs. But we must go beyond simply depending on God to help us survive while still operating within the world's systems and learn to depend on Him to be our Source which supersedes the circumstances of our world. We must be a people who live from the storehouses of God, together.

In the world we will see difficult and even dark times increase. There will be times when we are thrust into uncertainties and challenges in society that we did not expect. As believers, we must have something of our own "Mayflower

Compact" together, a government that lives through us in one accord, from the inside-out.

It's a government that actually increases in light, love, and peace even when our society or circumstances are most bleak. This is not a doomsday prophecy; rather, the Bible often talks about light and darkness, hope and difficulty, tribulations and joy put together at the same time. Increase will often go both ways at once. While darkness increases in the world, we must recognize that such are the exact times that God has prepared the increase of His government and peace through us as well. I tend to believe that darkness is the usher who shows light to its seat of destiny. We must be ready to take our seat and usher in the overcoming nature of our Lord and His government that lives in us.

> **"Arise, shine; for your light has come! And the glory of the Lord is risen upon you. For behold, the darkness shall cover the earth, and deep darkness the people; but the Lord will arise over you and His glory will be seen upon you." (Isaiah 60:1-2)**

> **"These things I have spoken to you, that in Me you may have peace. In the world you will have tribulation; but be of good cheer, I have overcome the world." (John 16:33)**

The increase of light is the only way to decrease the darkness; no legislation can do that by itself. An increase in our generosity will mean a decrease in dependence upon taxes. An increase in love will mean a decrease in the pandemic of fear. An increase in our uncommon unity will mean a decrease in the division of our time.

During times of trouble, people will flock to where there is hope. In the day to day, a great number of citizens find their hope in what the government does or what legislation they do or do not pass. We need to make sure that we as believers, as the church—and certainly not just *in* church—are the ones with the most hope; *we certainly should be.*

If we increase our hope no matter the circumstance, no matter what increase of difficulty or darkness is upon us, we will have the opportunity to increase His government here on earth as it is in heaven. We have to depend on a higher source of government so that we are not moved or shaken during tribulation. Then we have to set ourselves up as a giver of hope during those times of trouble—and at all times, really—so that we're not just one more person in line waiting and hoping for answers, but we are taking what we have in our hands, believing God, and joining in one accord with others.

Then, freely, generously give and watch hope multiply. A government of hope will mean that we are someone, somewhere, in whom the people know they will find the most hope.

The Way of Increase

To see this government fully come to life to serve the world and glorify our King we have to understand what this increase looks like through the eyes, and words, of the Son whose shoulders it was born upon. We go down to go up. The last become first. We often go back to go forward. We live inside-out. The weak are made strong and the meek inherit the earth. This is where the increase will be actualized, when we consistently live with a value system that lives these counter-cultural truths in deed, and not just in word or remembrance. These revolutionary Biblical principles of increase must become our new day-to-day standard of thinking, measuring, living, and giving; and then we will have ourselves a government of hope for which the world can leave its politics behind.

There's a story from December 8th in the devotional **Streams in the Desert** (*L.B. Cowman*) that simply and practically displays how we can take what we have in our hands and use it to bring increase wherever we go. It's one of my mom's favorites:

> *"There is an old story of an elderly man who always carried a little can of oil with him everywhere he went, and when he would go through a door that squeaked, he would squirt a little oil on the hinges. If he encountered a gate that was hard to open, he would oil the latch. And so he went through life, lubricating all the difficult places, making it easier for all those who came after him. People called the man eccentric, strange, and crazy, but he went steadily on, often refilling his can of oil when it was nearly empty, and oiling all the difficult places."*

There are creaky doors and hinges all over the world, most of which are waiting for the government to set things in place for them. There are opportunities both small and big all around us every day to release His government, to give what no other government really can. The way of increase is to be like this man with his oil can; or like the widow with only one jar of oil left. When we begin to pour out our oil on all the creaky hinges or in empty vessels, when we take what we have in our hands and consistently give it freely to the world, and when we all start living this way intentionally, together; that is when we will begin to multiply into a government of hope.

Some of us have money, some have time, some have talents, and some have a business or a non-profit organization; some have a church or a well-connected community around them.

What if we took whatever it is that we have, every day, and decided "you know what, I'm going to be the government for someone today." What if we looked for creaky doors and squeaky hinges, knowing that we carry a justice of grace for them that socialism does not need to fill. And it won't have a chance to do so if we have already stepped up to the plate.

I'm not talking about more ministries, more events, etc. I'm talking about the church, the family structure of people, coming into one heart and one mind with one another, each in their own way, and deciding that they will be the increase that knows no end. And just remember, when we see an increase in need or trouble in the world, if we haven't already, that's our cue to bring the increase of His government for the world to get in line to receive.

...And Peace

"Of the increase of His government and peace there will be no end..." (Isaiah 9:7)

"Blessed are the peacemakers, for they shall be called sons of God." (Matthew 5:9)

"For I declare that the sufferings of this present time are not worthy to be compared with the glory which shall be revealed in us. For the earnest expectation of the creation eagerly waits for the revealing of the sons of God. For the creation was subjected to futility, not willingly, but because of Him who subjected it in hope." (Romans 8:18-20)

I believe these three passages together tell us a prophetic story of the time we're living in and what the increase of God's government of hope will look like through us. First, we remember this word spoken over Jesus as He entered the world with a promise, carrying a government, *and a peace*, that would know no end. Those two are tied together. We've talked about the nature of God's government from the beginning of time being *family*. And in the Beatitudes Jesus continues to connect the dots when He blesses the peacemakers as the children of God, essentially saying that the arising government of our Everlasting Father's sons and daughters will be peacemakers.

Fast forward to the book of Romans and again we have that tension of increased present suffering but also the promise of increased glory to which the suffering can't compare. We're told that creation was subjected to futility because of God who subjected it in *HOPE*!

All along, the plan was to lead through the troubled times but for the sake of *HOPE*! And who will be carrying this hope of our Lord? Who is creation waiting and crying out for? None other than the sons and daughters of God, *for the family government of God*! And who are these sons and daughters? Jesus told us clearly—*they're the peacemakers*!

The world may know increased trouble in the days ahead, and we may not be able to depend upon our government to give us the answers we're accustomed to. But God has prepared by His Son, *in us*, a government of hope for which creation is crying out. This government of hope is His family, His sons and daughters, who will rise onto the scene as blessed peacemakers, carrying in them and reviving for the world around them a government *and* peace that will know no end.

We can depend on God for and provide for others what earthly governments cannot. Let's look again at this increased peace that is such a defining factor of the government of His sons and daughters: His Shalom.

As we talked about at the beginning of the book in regards to the Prince of Peace being such a vital branch of God's government, let's refresh what that means for us here.

Shalom = Completeness, wholeness, peace, health, welfare, safety, soundness, tranquility, prosperity, perfectness, fullness, rest, harmony; the absence of agitation or discord. Shalom comes from the root verb shalam, meaning 'to be complete, perfect and full.' *"It is the wholeness the entire human race seeks." (Strongs #7965, description from the New Spirit Filled Life Bible, Word Wealth: Nahum 1:15)*

These descriptions are the very things we line up for the government to supply for us, or even what we look for a good economy to provide. Neither of those are lasting for our dependence. The world is going to need these things even more than ever as we enter a time of "increase." While the world experiences increased tribulation or turmoil, we can give them increased shalom that will not end. We can give them what the government will not be able to: *"Completeness, wholeness, peace, health, welfare, safety, soundness, tranquility, prosperity, perfectness, fullness, rest, harmony; the absence of agitation or discord."*

With what we each have in our hands—our time, talents and treasures—and God's help to multiply, together we will not just provide for needs but empower people through them. We can be the family structure that gives something for the physical needs to stick to. We can be a living representation of hope. Most government programs breed dependence; but God's government through us should breed hope. We can be the church or pastor who dreams of partnering with others to open up free healthcare or childcare to the community. We can be the business that gives opportunities of vision and purpose to the hungry. We can be the fathers and mothers to the foster care system. We can be a non-profit that rallies others like them to come together and solve a homelessness crisis. We can be a government of hope!

This is our call, to be the increase of His government and peace that will know no end. None of us carry the whole on our own, and we have to be operating outside the walls of our physical structures, having become a *Family Structure* that is a storehouse of God for the world. This is the new world we are entering and as we disembark from our "Mayflower," we have this covenant-type government waiting for us to step into— *together*!

The Beginning

So let's disembark into this new world while girding up our perspective with a revolutionary mindset, let's covenant together in a renewed form of government that Jesus carried into the world in that most humble, Servant-Ruler way. Let's build a family structure greater and further-reaching than any physical structure ever could be by itself. Let's empower and build our house from the bottom, up, coming together in one heart and one soul, giving freely and generously while truly depending on the higher Source to be our new beginning.

Let's step into the role of Isaac and believe in the next generation to do the same, transforming people and nations through identity, building a holistic culture of life that supports and empowers free, good choices and ushering in the increase that our infant Savior brought us from heaven to earth, born into such humble circumstances. It's an increase that will know no end. *This is our beginning...*

Chapter 10:

Your Turn

"You are our epistle written in our hearts, known and read by all men..." (2 Corinthians 3:2)

It is your turn to write this chapter with your life across your community, culture or nation. You are a living epistle; you are His increase in this world. You are Chapter 10. Let's begin...together!

To join us in writing Chapter 10, please visit us at:

Facebook Group: Government of Hope – Chapter 10
Website: Governmentofhope.org

Thank you, and God bless you!

Chapter 10: Notes

Chapter 10: Notes

Chapter 10: Notes

End Notes:

General: All Biblical scripture citations are from the following, unless otherwise noted: New King James Version (Copyright 1982 by Thomas Nelson, Inc.) Used by Permission. All rights reserved.

Chapter 1:

Shalom: Strong's Concordance #7965
Word Wealth Description: New Spirit Filled Life Bible, Thomas Nelson Bibles. 2002.

Chapter 2:

Amazing Grace – Movie, directed by Michael Apted, 2006. (Los Angeles, CA: 20th Century Fox Home Entertainment, 2007)

U.S. History.org – William Penn

Biography.com, Author: Biography.com
Article title: William Penn Biography

LeTourneau, Joey. *Dream, Again*, pgs. 3, 104-105. (Imagi-Nations, LLC, 2013)

Chapter 3:

History.com: Mayflower Compact. By A&E Television
Article title: The Mayflower

Johnson. Bill. *Dreaming with God*
(Shippensburg, PA. Destiny Image Publishers. 2006)

Chapter 4:

LeTourneau, Joey. *If God Had A House*, Pgs. 11-12.
(ifgodhadahouse.com. 2017)

Chapter 5:

Finding Neverland. Directed by Marc Forster.
Miramax Films, 17 Dec. 2004.

Chapter 6:

LeTourneau, Joey. *The Power of Uncommon Unity*, Pgs. 127-128
(Shippensburg, PA: Destiny Image Publishers, 2013.)

Peterson, Eugene H. *The Message: The Bible in Contemporary Language*.
(Colorado Springs, CO. NavPress, 2002)

Chapter 7:

LeTourneau, Joey. *The Life Giver*, Pgs. 141-144.
(Shippensburg, PA: Destiny Image Publishers, 2012)

Chapter 9:

L.B. Cowman, Edited by James Reimann. *Streams in the Desert.*
(Grand Rapids, MI. Zondervan. 1997) Pgs. 455-456

Other Titles By Joey LeTourneau

Revolutionary Freedom

The Life Giver

The Power of Uncommon Unity

Dream, Again

Love Sees Differently

If God Had A House